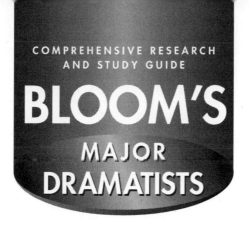

COMPREHENSIVE RESEARCH
AND STUDY GUIDE

BLOOM'S
MAJOR
DRAMATISTS

Tom Stoppard

EDITED AND WITH AN
INTRODUCTION BY HAROLD BLOOM

CURRENTLY AVAILABLE

BLOOM'S MAJOR DRAMATISTS

Aeschylus
Aristophanes
Bertolt Brecht
Anton Chekhov
Euripides
Henrik Ibsen
Eugène Ionesco
Ben Jonson
Christopher Marlowe
Arthur Miller
Molière
Eugene O'Neill
Luigi Pirandello
Shakespeare's Comedies
Shakespeare's Histories
Shakespeare's Romances
Shakespeare's Tragedies
George Bernard Shaw
Sam Shepard
Neil Simon
Sophocles
Tom Stoppard
Oscar Wilde
Thornton Wilder
Tennessee Williams
August Wilson

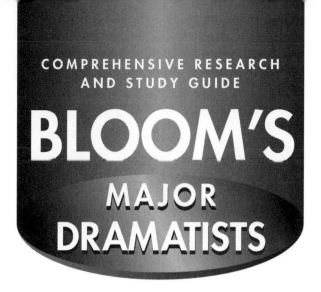

COMPREHENSIVE RESEARCH
AND STUDY GUIDE

BLOOM'S
MAJOR
DRAMATISTS

Tom
Stoppard

EDITED AND WITH AN INTRODUCTION
BY HAROLD BLOOM

CHELSEA HOUSE
PUBLISHERS
A Haights Cross Communications Company
Philadelphia

© 2003 by Chelsea House Publishers, a subsidiary of
Haights Cross Communications.

A Haights Cross Communications  Company

Introduction © 2003 by Harold Bloom.

Printed and bound in the United States of America.

First Printing
1 3 5 7 9 8 6 4 2

Library of Congress Cataloging-in-Publication Data applied for.

ISBN 0-7910-7032-8

Chelsea House Publishers
1974 Sproul Road, Suite 400
Broomall, PA 19008-0914

http://www.chelseahouse.com

Contributing Editor: Jocelyn Stauffer

Cover design by Terry Mallon

Layout by EJB Publishing Services

CONTENTS

USER'S GUIDE

This volume is designed to present biographical, critical, and bibliographical information on the author and the author's best-known or most important plays. Following Harold Bloom's editor's note and introduction is a concise biography of the author that discusses major life events and important literary accomplishments. A critical analysis of each play follows, tracing significant themes, patterns, and motifs in the work. An annotated list of characters supplies brief information on the main characters in each play.

A selection of critical extracts, derived from previously published material, follows each thematic analysis. In most cases, these extracts represent the best analysis available from a number of leading critics. Because these extracts are derived from previously published material, they will include the original notations and references when available. Each extract is cited, and readers are encouraged to use the original publications as they continue their research. A bibliography of the author's writings, a list of additional books and articles on the author and their work, and an index of themes and ideas conclude the volume.

As with any study guide, this volume is designed as a supplement to the works being discussed, and is in no way intended as a replacement for those works. The reader is advised to read the text prior to using this study guide, and to keep it accessible for quick reference.

ABOUT THE EDITOR

Harold Bloom is Sterling Professor of the Humanities at Yale University and Henry W. and Albert A. Berg Professor of English at the New York University Graduate School. He is the author of over 20 books, and the editor of more than 30 anthologies of literary criticism.

Professor Bloom's works include *Shelley's Mythmaking* (1959), *The Visionary Company* (1961), *Blake's Apocalypse* (1963), *Yeats* (1970), *A Map of Misreading* (1975), *Kabbalah and Criticism* (1975), *Agon: Toward a Theory of Revisionism* (1982), *The American Religion* (1992), *The Western Canon* (1994), and *Omens of Millennium: The Gnosis of Angels, Dreams, and Resurrection* (1996). *The Anxiety of Influence* (1973) sets forth Professor Bloom's provocative theory of the literary relationships between the great writers and their predecessors. His most recent books include *Shakespeare: The Invention of the Human*, a 1998 National Book Award finalist, *How to Read and Why* (2000), and *Genius: A Mosaic of One Hundred Exemplary Creative Minds* (2002).

Professor Bloom earned his Ph.D. from Yale University in 1955 and has served on the Yale faculty since then. He is a 1985 MacArthur Foundation Award recipient and served as the Charles Eliot Norton Professor of Poetry at Harvard University in 1987–88. In 1999 he was awarded the prestigious American Academy of Arts and Letters Gold Medal for Criticism. Professor Bloom is the editor of several other Chelsea House series in literary criticism, including BLOOM'S MAJOR SHORT STORY WRITERS, BLOOM'S MAJOR NOVELISTS, BLOOM'S MAJOR DRAMATISTS, BLOOM'S MODERN CRITICAL INTERPRETATIONS, BLOOM'S MODERN CRITICAL VIEWS, and BLOOM'S BIOCRITIQUES.

EDITOR'S NOTE

My Introduction centers upon *The Invention of Love*, and tries to restore the aesthetic balance between A.E. Housman and Oscar Wilde, whom Stoppard seems to favor.

C.W.E. Bigsby takes the honors on *Rosencrantz and Guildenstern Are Dead*, with his exaltation of absurdity.

On *Jumpers*, a mixed bag of a play, I prefer Paul Delaney on the Stoppardian moral relativism.

Travesties, a superb invention, is shrewdly seen by Anthony Jenkins as a triumph of style over content.

Arcadia, a baroque splendor, is read by Hersh Zeifman as a dialectic of sex and chaos.

John Fleming sets forth the conflict of Housman versus Wilde, more or less in Stoppard's own terms, from which I dissent in my Introduction.

Harold Bloom

The Invention of Love seems to me Tom Stoppard's masterpiece to date. He long ago transcended the influence of Samuel Beckett, which still clouds (for me) *Rosencrantz and Guildenstern Are Dead*. His true precursor has become the divine Oscar Wilde, and one feels that if another *Importance of Being Earnest* ever is going to be composed, it will be by Stoppard.

Unless I misread Stoppard (always possible with so great an ironist) the closing contrast between A.E. Housman and Oscar Wilde is not much to Housman's credit. Wilde lived and loved; Housman stayed home and avoided scandal. For Stoppard, these are questions of success or failure. But are they?

What has happened to the Aesthetic in a play about the Aesthetic Movement, whose high priest, the sublime Walter Pater, is badly travestied in Stoppard's play? Would you know from Stoppard that Oscar rarely had an idea that was not vulgarized from Pater?

Housman however is the point, because he was a great poet, as you could not know from reading *The Invention of Love*. Try the effect of reading just four or five lyrics by Housman, in the midst of your reading *The Invention of Love*. They might include some of my favorites: "Into my heart an air that kills," "Eight O'Clock," "The Night is Freezing Fast," and the lovely "Tell me not here, it needs not saying." Or try a more radical experiment. Read against Stoppard's play, as counterpoint, Housman's magnificent and perpetually relevant "Epitaph On an Army of Mercenaries:"

> These, in the day when heaven was falling,
>   The hour when earth's foundations fled,
> Followed their mercenary calling
>   And took their wages and are dead.
>
> Their shoulders held the sky suspended;
>   They stood, and earth's foundations stay;
> What God abandoned, these defended,
>   And saved the sum of things for pay.

Housman, a great classical scholar, has written an epitaph worthy of Simonides. But my interest is elsewhere. Did Stoppard's Housman write this strong and uncompromising poem? Heaven always is falling, and earth's foundations perpetually flee away. All callings are mercenary, whether Oxford dons or dramatists or what you will. We are all God's mercenaries, Housman suggests, and must defend what He abandoned. *The Invention of Love* is an admirable play, but hardly just to the poet Housman, whose difficult, evasive poetry also saved the sum of things for pay.

BIOGRAPHY OF

Tom Stoppard

Tom Stoppard was born Tomáš Sträusslcr on July 3, 1937 in Zlín, Czechoslovakia (now the Czech Republic), the second son of Dr. Eugen Sträussler, a physician for the Bata shoe company, and his wife Martha. On March 14, 1939, the day the Nazis invaded Czechoslovakia, his family fled to Singapore with other Jewish doctors that had worked for Bata. In Singapore, Tomáš briefly attended an English convent school. Shortly thereafter, before the Japanese invasion, he was evacuated with his mother and brother from Singapore to India. His father stayed behind and was killed. Tomáš was only four years old at the time.

In Darjeeling, he attended school while his mother managed the local Bata shoe store. Several years later, his mother married Kenneth Stoppard, a British Army major in India. The family moved to England and Major Stoppard adopted Tomáš and his brother, giving them his last name—Tomáš Sträussler became Tom Stoppard. After leaving Czechoslovakia (which he doesn't remember), Singapore (which he only vaguely recalls) and India (which he has fond memories of), he finally had a permanent home in England and started to identify with and embrace his Britishness.

Although he's been criticized for writing overly clever and erudite plays, Stoppard never attended college. After a prep school education, he opted to drop out at age seventeen due to academic boredom. He obtained a job as a journalist for the *Western Daily Press* in 1954, where he wanted to be a field reporter in world "hot spots," but instead wrote news, features, and play and film reviews. He switched to the *Bristol Evening World* in 1958 as his interest in theater was growing. The London theater scene was ripe at that point: critics have variously pointed to Peter O'Toole's stellar performance as Hamlet, Thomas Beckett's *Waiting for Godot*, John Osborne's *Look Back in Anger*, Peter Hall's directing, and Kenneth Tynan's insightful theater reviews as having injected British theater with vitality.

In 1960, at the age of 23, Stoppard decided to quit journalism and attempt a career as a playwright. His first work was *A Walk on the Water* (televised in 1963). While he was writing (*The Gamblers* and several unproduced television plays), he had a brief stint as a theater critic for London's *Scene* magazine. He wrote *Rosencrantz and Guildenstern Meet King Lear*—the seed for a play that would eventually become his career-making *Rosencrantz and Guildenstern Are Dead*—in 1964 while in Berlin on a Ford Foundation Grant. Between 1966 and 1968, *Rosencrantz and Guildenstern Are Dead* was performed first at the Edinburgh Festival Fringe, then at the National Theatre (making him the youngest playwright to have a play performed there), and finally on Broadway, where it won the Tony for best play in 1968. Because of the critical windfall, he became famous nearly overnight. His other works were staged—or broadcast on radio or TV—during this time. His only novel, *Lord Malquist and Mr. Moon*, was published in 1966. The characters in this novel—Lord Malquist as the callous dandy and Mr. Moon as the unfortunate innocent to whom bad things happen—appear in a few of his early works by personality, if not by name (although the name "Moon" was used in several of his works). Stoppard has identified himself as being a "Moon," although some critics would argue that he's more a "Malquist."

Even from his earliest works, there are signature Stoppard elements that were to become his trademarks. Stoppard admits that his plays often don't make a single, clear statement, relying instead on what he describes as 'firstly, A; secondly minus A.' A statement may be made by one character that conflicts with the statement of another, setting up Stoppard's 'infinite leapfrog.' Critics also charged that his plays and characters were too steeped in intellectualism, another Stoppard trademark. Later in his career, critics noted that his characters became more fully developed and emotional. Stoppard has stated that as he grows older, he conceals himself less and his writing has become more a product of his true self.

In 1965, he married Jose Ingle, a nurse, with whom he has two sons, Oliver and Barnaby. Between 1969 and 1972, he divorced Jose, gained custody of their two sons, and married medical doctor/author/TV personality, Dr. Miriam Moore-Robinson. Together they have two sons, William and Edmund.

Several of Stoppard's plays were produced in New York in the mid-seventies: *Jumpers*, *Enter a Free Man*, and *Travesties*, which won two Tony Awards, including Best Play in 1976. Also in 1976 he became politically involved and began speaking out on behalf of Soviet dissidents. His meeting with Victor Fainberg, who was institutionalized for protesting the Czech invasion, led to *Every Good Boy Deserves Favour*, a musical collaboration with André Previn. And, for the 1980 Olympics, Stoppard supported the boycott movement due to the Soviet treatment of dissidents.

The early eighties marked the start of Tom Stoppard's close association with actress Felicity Kendal, who starred in many of his plays. Onstage, she played the leading roles of Dotty in *Jumpers*, Flora Crewe in *Indian Ink*, and Hannah Jarvis in *Arcadia*, among others. Offstage, by 1990, they were romantically linked in a relationship that would last eight years; in 1991, he dedicated *In the Native State* to her. His divorce from Miriam Stoppard was finalized in 1992.

Stoppard's screenplay for *Brazil* received an Oscar nomination in 1985. Other screenplays followed, such as *Empire of the Sun*, which was directed by Steven Spielberg. He didn't receive credit for, but made contributions to, the screenplays of *Always* and *Indiana Jones and the Last Crusade*. He was credited with *The Russia House*, *Billy Bathgate* and *Shakespeare in Love* screenplays. The latter won three Golden Globes (including best screenplay) and seven Oscars (including best screenplay and best picture in 1999, seven years after Stoppard and Marc Norman wrote it).

In 1993, *Arcadia* was staged at the National Theatre and broadcast on the radio. Two years later, it was nominated for a Tony Award for best play. Stoppard began to accumulate other high honors. In 1978, he received a CBE (Commander of the British Empire) and the Queen knighted him in 1997, making him the first dramatist since 1971 to be given such a distinction—Tomáš Straüssler, who had become Tom Stoppard, became Sir Tom Stoppard in 1997. In 2000, he received the Order of Merit, a personal honor from the Queen, and the French Government honored him as an Officier de l'Ordre des Arts et des Lettres.

In the mid-nineties, Stoppard was surprised to discover through a Czech relative that his family had been Jewish and several of his family members had perished in the Holocaust. He and his brother Peter returned to their birthplace in 1998 for the first time since their family fled in 1939.

In his celebrated life as a writer, Tom Stoppard has been a journalist, a playwright, a screenwriter, a radio and TV writer, an adapter, and more. In 1974, he even called himself a writer 'for hire.' His most recent work is a trilogy of plays set in nineteenth-century Russia called *The Coast of Utopia*.

PLOT SUMMARY OF

Rosencrantz and Guildenstern Are Dead

Whereas Rosencrantz and Guildenstern are minor characters in Shakespeare's *Hamlet*, they are elevated to lead roles in Stoppard's *Rosencrantz and Guildenstern Are Dead*. Throughout the play, Ros and Guil (as they are referred to in the script) reenact the plots, structure, and entire scenes from *Hamlet*. We, as the audience, recognize the famous storyline of *Hamlet*, but, as characters within a different play, Ros and Guil aren't aware of the framework in which they exist. In keeping with Shakespeare's version of Rosencrantz and Guildenstern, though, this Ros and Guil are likewise doomed, as the play's title spells out.

From the beginning of the play, the audience is clued into the artificiality of Ros and Guil's world, as Rosencrantz flips a coin which has landed "heads up" over ninety times. Guildenstern is puzzled as to why the tossing isn't following mathematical rules. Then, both men suddenly remember they were woken by a messenger that morning and they are supposed to be on important official business.

A band of performers arrives and offers to perform any kind of tragedy for a fee. The Player—the spokesman of the group of Tragedians—offers to perform the *Rape of the Sabine Women* with the young actor Alfred in a skirt. Guildenstern, appalled, slaps the Player and decries the troupe as a pornographer with his prostitutes. The Player engages in a coin-tossing game with Guildenstern and loses all his money.

The scene is interrupted with characters from *Hamlet*. Claudius the king, with Gertrude his queen, enter and greet Ros and Guil. Claudius wants Rosencrantz and Guildenstern— Hamlet's closest friends—to make Hamlet happy and determine what is troubling him.

Directionless and alone, Ros and Guil wish to be home. They banter and play word games until Hamlet crosses behind them and leaves. To learn the cause of Hamlet's "insanity," Rosencrantz fires questions at Guildenstern, who answers as if he were Hamlet. In the exchange, Guildenstern-as-Hamlet states that his father was once king; when the king suddenly died, Hamlet's uncle succeeded his brother on the throne, marrying Hamlet's mother. They reason that this is the cause of the change in Hamlet's behavior. The real Hamlet then enters and greets his friends.

At the beginning of Act Two, Hamlet manages to tell his friends that he is only partly mad, but Rosencrantz and Guildenstern feel as if they were stymied in their attempts to delve deeper into his psyche. Hamlet lingers to ask the Player if he can perform *The Murder of Gonzago* and include a change that he himself will write.

The Player replies that actors—"the opposite of people"— need an audience and their own audiences had become sparse. *The Murder of Gonzago*, the planned play, is about a King and Queen, and themes including blood, love and rhetoric. Rosencrantz and Guildenstern are still directionless, but the Player tells them to relax, respond and act natural. Further, he asks them what they assume about Hamlet. Rosencrantz and Guildenstern assume that he is actually sane.

The Player reveals the king thinks Hamlet is in love with Polonius' daughter Ophelia. The conversation switches to the subject of death—a recurring motif both in *Hamlet* and in this play. Claudius leaves with Gertrude, but before he exits, he says Hamlet has been sent for so that he can be with Ophelia "by accident."

Hamlet and Ophelia do meet up and walk together, talking. That leaves Rosencrantz and Guildenstern alone to watch the dress rehearsal for the play Hamlet commissioned, which re-tells the tragic story of the king being poisoned by his brother (Prince Hamlet's uncle), and the brother subsequently taking over the kingdom and marrying the king's widow. The dress rehearsal ends and Hamlet and Ophelia enter. Ophelia drops to the floor sobbing as Hamlet yells at her hysterically. He implies that either the king or queen will die. Claudius enters and pulls Ophelia to her feet. He says that Hamlet is not mad; nor does he love her. Claudius intends to send him to England.

The players resume their dress rehearsal for Act II of the play-within-the-play, which is the culmination of tragedy: those that are "marked for death" will die. A love scene between the poisoner and the widow bothers Rosencrantz, who protests that the audience is not interested in such filth; the Player insists that they are in fact entertained by murder, seduction and incest. Rosencrantz prefers a straightforward story in a logical progression of beginning, middle and end, while Guildenstern wants art to reflect life.

The play continues and foreshadows future events, including a mime of the nephew's (Hamlet's) "madness," a confrontation with his mother the queen, his stabbing of Polonius and his eventual banishment to England accompanied by two friends. In the mime, when they reach England, the king orders the friends' deaths. As the Tragedians portray the two friends/spies, Rosencrantz and Guildenstern see that the actors' costumes look familiar, but fail to connect the fate of the characters with themselves. The Tragedians fall to the ground, feigning the death of the spies. The Player says that death and killing is the talent of actors. Giving voice to the play's running commentary on acting versus reality, Guildenstern counters that falling to one's knees and gasping is not death.

The sun rises and Rosencrantz and Guildenstern are sprawled on the ground in the same spot as the actors had been. The actions that were prophesized in the play start to come to fruition: Hamlet does stab Polonius; the king and queen find out and ask Rosencrantz and Guildenstern to bring Hamlet to them. The two friends see Hamlet dragging Polonius' body, but their hesitation and inaction allow him to get away. Hamlet returns; the king approaches and Hamlet and his friends bow. With their heads low, they do not notice that Hamlet does an about-face and escapes briefly before being caught again and made to follow the king. Rosencrantz and Guildenstern are going to accompany Hamlet to England. Hamlet, in fact, tells them that they can go. Rosencrantz feels that this means anything could happen.

As Act Three opens, Rosencrantz and Guildenstern are in darkness, surrounded by the sounds of the sea. They're not sure what to think and don't know where they are; their continual waiting and lack of action recalls Samuel Beckett's play, *Waiting for Godot*. Hamlet lights a lantern and all are revealed to be on a boat. The sea carries the boat along as the action of the play continues on board. Rosencrantz and Guildenstern still have their mission, though, to take Hamlet to England and convey a letter to the English king. Guildenstern accuses Rosencrantz of repeating everything he says; Rosencrantz protests that Guildenstern must be the "dominant personality" because he is better as a supporting character. They talk again of the letter for the king and eventually Guildenstern produces it from his pocket.

They talk of death—not the death that the Tragedians show, but the "not-being," as Guildenstern says. Ripping open the letter, they read that it gives orders to cut off Hamlet's head. They weigh their options and decide to do nothing. (Importantly, this was their one chance to take action and to break free of *Hamlet*'s constraints, which they fail to do). Hamlet overhears their conversation, waits for them to fall asleep, edits the letter and replaces it.

When the sun rises the next morning, Rosencrantz and Guildenstern hear music (a recorder) playing. Rosencrantz follows the source to three barrels. A drum and lute join in with the recorder and play a tune associated with the Tragedians. All the Tragedians pop out of the barrels and say that they are traveling because the king didn't like the play they performed. Hamlet walks to the edge of the stage and spits at the theater audience.

Pirates attack the boat and Hamlet, Rosencrantz, Guildenstern, and the Player jump into the three barrels. Hamlet's barrel disappears and Ros and Guil assume he's dead to them (e.g. not coming back). They are again without direction, as their mission and their letter were dependent on Hamlet. Guildenstern rips open the letter and finds that it orders their death instead of Hamlet's. The Player rallies his Tragedians, who form a menacing circle around Ros and Guil.

Guildenstern, dismissing the "casual deaths" of actors, grabs a dagger from the Player's belt and plunges it into the Player's throat. The Player dies; the Tragedians applaud. His death by stage dagger was merely acted. The Tragedians form a death tableau and mimic Ros and Guil's eventual death by stabbing, along with the king and queen, ala *Hamlet*. Guildenstern's last line is "Well, we'll know better next time. Now you see me, now you—." He disappears. The lights go up on a scene that replicates the Tragedians' version of the death tableau, this time substituting the *Hamlet* characters.

The original ending of the play features a speech by Fortinbras, who bids that the bodies be taken away. When they are, two Ambassadors list the eight corpses: Claudius, Gertrude, Hamlet, Laertes, Rosencrantz, Guildenstern, Polonius, and Ophelia. In the distance, there is the sound of banging on a wooden door and two incomprehensible names being called (paralleling Ros and Guil's call). The ambassadors go to investigate as the Tragedian's tune is heard in the distance and theater's house lights come up.

In the second edition's ending, two English ambassadors arrive to report that Rosencrantz and Guildenstern are dead. As the lights fade, Horatio (from *Hamlet*) holds Hamlet and tells the ambassadors that the orders were not to kill Rosencrantz and Guildenstern. He offers to tell all the events that led up to this death scene as the theater's stage goes black.

Rosencrantz and Guildenstern Are Dead

Rosencrantz is the down-to-earth, somewhat obtuse and reactive member of the Elizabethan duo. He's the character who *feels*. Innocent and kind almost to a fault, he tries on several occasions to cheer Guildenstern and feels "a little embarrassed" to win his money at their coin-tossing games. In his own words, he feels he's the supporting character and that Guildenstern is the dominant personality. Tellingly, when he and Guildenstern know that the king's letter commands that Hamlet should be killed, Rosencrantz defends Hamlet, saying that they are his friends and protests that he's done nothing to them—but still, he listens to Guildenstern and does nothing because he is the one that is led.

Guildenstern, by contrast, is the leader and the thinking member of the duo. It is he who notices that the coin-tossing isn't adhering to mathematical principles and tries to puzzle *why*. Stoppard described his titular pair of characters as being "two halves of the same personality," so it follows that Guildenstern is the more poetic and philosophical of the two, given to spouting stage-y dialogue. Because he can generally sense when something is wrong, he worries about it. Whereas Rosencrantz's earthiness makes him susceptible to the temptations of The Player and his troupe's more suggestive repertoire, Guildenstern is disgusted by them. He is more concerned with culture and would like art to imitate life.

The Player is the leader of a band of wandering actors who call themselves, "The Tragedians." His sardonic, confident nature contrasts with Rosencrantz and Guildenstern's uncertainty. Accepting his "role" in life, he confidently doesn't question what goes on around him, because he's content to act. He does, however, always need an audience and his troupe's repertoire offers diversions for every taste. He's not a kind person—in particular, he mistreats Alfred—and he tries to cheat Rosencrantz and Guildenstern.

Hamlet, the prince of Denmark, has been relegated from the major role in Shakespeare's play to the minor character he is in this play. Indeed, he is nearly the sketch of a character that Ros and Guil were in *Hamlet*. He is moody and distracted (given that his uncle killed his father and married his mother), but calculating in his pretend "madness." He has The Player and his troupe perform the *Murder at Gonzago* play with changes made to allude to Claudius' treachery. He stabs Polonius. And, given the opportunity, he saves his own life by switching the letter that condemned him with the orders that that his friends Rosencrantz and Guildenstern should be killed instead.

Claudius, the king of Denmark, is lecherous. He killed his brother the king, married his brother's widow, assumed the throne and kingdom that belonged to Hamlet, and plotted to kill Hamlet. He sends for Hamlet's friends Rosencrantz and Guildenstern to cheer Hamlet, although he confuses the two men and eventually orders their deaths.

Gertrude, the queen of Denmark, doesn't seem to know what's going on around her and doesn't know why Hamlet is moody. Tellingly, she seems to just be a "dress," instead of a character, as Rosencrantz mistakes Alfred wearing a dress for the queen.

Alfred, a Tragedian, wears a skirt and is offered by The Player to portray *The Rape of the Sabine Women*. When asked, he admits that he doesn't like being an actor and breaks down in sniffles.

Ophelia is the object of Hamlet's affection.

Polonius, Ophelia's father and Claudius' advisor, is killed by Hamlet.

Rosencrantz and Guildenstern Are Dead

C. W. E. BIGSBY ON ABSURDITY

[C. W. E. Bigsby is Professor of American Studies at the University of East Anglia, whose published works include books on contemporary American drama, Dada and Surrealism, and Edward Albee. Although he identifies elements of absurdity in the play in this excerpt, he does not go as far as to say that Stoppard is an absurdist.]

Is Stoppard, then, an absurdist? Like most arbitrary categories this is frequently more misleading than helpful, as has proved the case with writers such as Pinter and Albee. Yet the iconography of *Rosencrantz and Guildenstern are Dead* is familiar to audiences who cut their critical teeth on Beckett and Ionesco. The absurdists captured a deracinated world—a world in which the potential for action and communication has been irrevocably eroded. The setting is timeless, the landscape an expressionistic desert reminiscent of Dali's lapidary wilderness[1] or the claustrophobic living room of modern, uncommunal living. The capacity for action is minimal and ironic. Language itself is simply an elaborate papering over of cracks, which constantly threaten to open up beneath those who remain either blithely unaware of their plight or numbed with despair. That anguish obviously exists in Stoppard's play—a work in which two men are seen 'passing the time in a place without any visible character', clinging fiercely to the conviction that they 'have not been picked out ... simply to be abandoned', that they are 'entitled to some direction', only to confess at the end of their 'play' that 'it is not enough. To be told so little—to such an end—and still, finally, to be denied an explanation.' The only resources available to these abandoned characters are the compassion with which they respond to one another and the humour which they deploy as a means of neutralizing their fear. Niebur's comment that laughter is a kind of no man's land between faith and despair is clearly applicable to *Rosencrantz and Guildenstern are Dead*. For Rosencrantz and Guildenstern themselves, humour is a means of preserving sanity; for Stoppard it is a natural product of disjunction—of the gulf between cause and effect, aspiration and fulfilment, word and meaning, which is the root alike of pain, absurdity, and laughter, and a clue to the relativity of truth, itself a subject to which Stoppard has repeatedly returned.

NOTE

1. The adjective refers to Dali's paintings, which often picture desolate landscapes, dominated by rocks and stones.

—C. W. E. Bigsby, *Tom Stoppard*, ed. Ian Scott-Kilvert, (Harlow [Eng.]: Published for the British Council by Longman Group, 1976): pp. 15–16.

LUCINA PAQUET GABBARD ON THE THEME OF DEATH

[Lucina Paquet Gabbard, Emeritus Professor of English at Eastern Illinois University, has published a book, *The Dream Structure of Pinter Plays—A Psychoanalytic Approach*, as well as a variety of articles on Stoppard, Pinter, Albee, and O'Neill. In this excerpt, Gabbard explores the theme of death and all the ways it is reinforced in the play.]

The end toward which they [Ros and Guil] drift is, of course, death—life's greatest mystery and the principal focus of this play. The *Hamlet* fragments within *Rosencrantz and Guildenstern Are Dead* bring into relief three facets of death. First, it is the certain end of life. Rosencrantz and Guildenstern sense this certainty from their first contact with *Hamlet*. In voicing his discomfort at Elsinore, Rosencrantz stammers that things are "stopping to a death" or "heading to a dead stop—" (p. 38). The final tableau illustrates that *all* life's characters do reach this same end. Indeed, this blunt inevitability sometimes makes death appear as a welcome release. Hamlet illustrates this wish for release by expressing his willingness to part from his life. Secondly, the dramatic structure of tragedy envelops death in a romantic aura. The hero has died bravely after a violent struggle. Even the antagonists have met death in action. The collected bodies are to be placed on a high stage for all to view while Horatio explains the mishaps that brought these things about. The spectator will leave feeling informed, purged, and uplifted. Moreover ·for a moment, through identification with Hamlet, he will have fantasized himself as witness to his own funeral.

The players' entertainments are also littered with death. Dying and killing are, in fact, their greatest talents. Between the two they do impart, like tragedy, the message that death is certain, for their plays never end while anyone is on his feet. Theirs is such an ancient tradition that the players themselves impart the sense that death is a developing process creeping over man, his fictions, and his world. On their first entrance, the Player explains that they are growing rusty and approaching decadence. Moments later he requests that his new-found audience not clap too loudly for the world is very old (p. 23). Unfortunately, the players make death a game. "The mechanics of cheap melodrama," Guildenstern calls it, incapable of catching people unawares and whispering into their skulls that they will die one day (p. 83). The Player's justification adds the interesting third note to the image of melodramatic death: it is what the people want. The Player says that audiences are only prepared to believe in what they expect (p. 84). At the end of the frame play, Guildenstern himself is taken in by the Player's stunning portrayal of death by stabbing (p. 123).

The Absurdist's mirror also shows death as a developing process that begins at birth. From the moment Rosencrantz and Guildenstern respond to the urgent royal summons, with no questions asked, they have stepped into the life that leads to death. The summons is a metaphor for both the beginning and the ending of life. The royal call in the pale sky before dawn is comparable to the involuntary event of birth set in progress by the king and queen of each child's life—his parents. The same summons raises the specter of death as the pale rider. To

Guildenstern, he was only "a hat and a cloak levitating in the grey plume of his own breath" (p. 39). By answering the call, Rosencrantz and Guildenstern begin death-in-life. Their passivity and inaction are appropriate to their decaying state. Somewhere in their confusion and uncertainty, they are dimly aware that body signs do not mean life. Rosencrantz reports that fingernails and beards grow after death (p. 18). Thus, the title of the frame play takes on new meaning—Rosencrantz and Guildenstern are dead from the outset, born into a deathly life without order or action. The boat image also takes on additional meaning. This is the ship that crosses the sea of death, carrying its souls to the "other side." This lifeless journey into the void is the only certainty and must be escaped through loss of memory. Rosencrantz has forgotten that shattering moment in his childhood when he first realized he was mortal.

Nevertheless, as this developing certainty becomes increasingly imminent, Rosencrantz and Guildenstern are forced to face its mysteries. Death is not the fantasy of witnessing one's own funeral; it is not like being *alive* inside a coffin. Nor is it a game from which corpses jump up for applause. Guildenstern defines it as "failing to reappear," as "an exit, unobtrusive and unannounced, a disappearance" (p. 84). It is a fearsome reality not to be forestalled. Eventually, however, as with Hamlet, their wish to escape from death metamorphoses into a wish to escape into death. Death begins to beckon; and when the opportunity comes to go free, Rosencrantz and Guildenstern reject it. The wish to know, to be released from fear and uncertainty, couples with their passivity and keeps them on their drifting course to eternity.

They do not, however, meet death romantically, as in *Hamlet*. They go out whimpering and uncomprehending: someone had it in for them; who would have thought they were so important; they should have been given an explanation (p. 122). Then they disappear as in their own definition, "Now you see me now you—" (p. 126). But Guildenstern doubts even his own existentialist vision; as he fades into not being, he hopes—he wishes for another chance, "Well, we'll know better next time" (p. 126).

Death folds into uncertainty, and together they form the chief emphasis of the complexity of ideas presented in this triptych. Moving back from the details of each panel allows the overall pattern of *Rosencrantz and Guildenstern Are Dead* to come into focus. Rosencrantz and Guildenstern are innocents, newborn to the journey of life by the recency of their summons and newborn to art as heroes of the latest drama in theatre's chronology. As they journey, they meet the players—the raggle-taggle of life and art, bedraggled by their longevity but surviving by their adaptability and willingness to please. They make a pair; Rosencrantz and Guildenstern are watchers and the players need an audience. Together they encounter *Hamlet* and get caught up in its action. *Hamlet*, with is superior sense of order, takes the role of divine authority, dictating the course of events leading to death. But within that order the ancients and the innocents maintain their own characters. The ancient players show the beginnings of life and drama in improvisation and responsiveness. *Hamlet* represents the order and design of maturity. The innocents give body to the disorder born of forgetfulness and the need to seek new forms. The three stages of life and drama, intermingled in the frame play, come to a halt before the mystery of death. Each presents its own view, but none speaks from experience. The timeless melodramas, by their distance from death, can afford to treat it as a game and a pretense. The ordered tragedies with their linear design take death seriously as an end to be faced and accepted. The disenchanted moderns, by their proximity to death, must blur it into an ambiguity, such as Godot. Is he death or is he God or is he salvation or is he—? Or they ignore it by viewing life as a circular pattern which blends ends into beginnings and looks forward to doing better next time. Moreover, death is made easier to ignore by corpses that disappear. In this twentieth century drama there are no remains—only space, empty but provocative. As history has progressively diminished the authority of God, so has drama become less a statement than a question. The final questions of the frame play emerge as multileveled as the play itself. Rosencrantz and Guildenstern ask: is there a next time? will life and drama be better? Their play asks: which of these mirrors reflects life and death most truly? is there one reality for all time? is there a God? And the questions multiply like the images created by three mirrors throwing their reflections one upon the other. (...)

As *Hamlet* and Absurdism come into contrast, the frame play seems to point clearly to one worthwhile aim of tragedy. It attempts to remind men not only that death is the certain end of life, but also that it does not necessarily operate by justice. Tragic irony teaches that the good end unluckily (p. 80). Rosencrantz and Guildenstern seem not to know this. They exist in tandem with Beckett's heroes who end paralyzed but still alive. They represent contemporary life where corpses disappear into mortuaries. They are, therefore, unprepared for death; they ask to "stay put" (p. 125). They are surprised to be taken since they are so innocent of wrongdoing (p. 125). They feel abused having to die without explanations (p. 122).

—Lucina Paquet Gabbard, *The Stoppard Plays*, (Troy, N.Y.: Whitston Pub. Co., 1982): pp. 33–36, 37.

RICHARD CORBALLIS ON THE ROLE OF ROS AND GUIL VERSUS THE TRAGEDIANS

[Richard Corballis is a Senior Lecturer in English at New Zealand's University of Canterbury who has written articles and reviews on Renaissance and modern drama and published books on John Webster and Thomas Dekker, among others. Here, he points to Ros and Guil as spectators, extensions of the audience who inhabit the "real" world, unlike the "artificial" world represented by the *Hamlet* cast. In contrast, the Tragedians start out being "real," but switch to being "artificial" during the course of the play.]

It is, I surmise, in order to emphasize their role as spectators that Stoppard has incorporated into his play scenes from *Hamlet* in which Rosencrantz and Guildenstern are spectators pure and simple. Time and again we find them downstage, observing the scenes from *Hamlet* which are going on upstage. At times they express their awareness of the passive role they are playing: 'I feel like a spectator', says Rosencrantz late in Act I. At other times they put this awareness to spectacular effect: 'Next!' shouts Rosencrantz in Act II, presumably imitating a director auditioning actors—a role more obviously assumed by Guildenstern much earlier, when he tells the miserable Alfred, 'We'll let you know'. All this seems to suggest that Stoppard regards Rosencrantz and Guildenstern as an extension of the audience. The pair deliver many of their speeches directly to the audience, the most spectacular case in point occurring in Act II when Rosencrantz yells, 'Fire!' at the audience and, when they don't move, observes contemptuously: 'They should burn to death in their shoes'. The published text is designed for performance in theatres with a proscenium arch and footlights; in more adaptable spaces I imagine Stoppard would approve if Rosencrantz and Guildenstern were to mingle with the audience on occasions, just as Moon and Birdboot do in *The Real Inspector Hound*.

This brings us back to the point that Rosencrantz and Guildenstern, on the one hand, and the cast of *Hamlet*, on the other, are strictly juxtaposed. Rosencrantz and Guildenstern are portrayed as an extension of the audience and therefore as 'real' people; the *Hamlet* characters, by virtue of the onstage audience (added to the offstage one), are made to appear all the more stagey, 'clockwork' and 'unreal'. It is noteworthy that on the one occasion when Hamlet tries to communicate with the audience he fails to penetrate the invisible fourth wall of the conventional stage:

> HAMLET *comes down to the footlights and regards the audience. The others watch but don't speak.* HAMLET *clears his throat noisily and spits into the audience. A split second later he claps his hand to his eye and wipes himself. He goes back upstage.*

The conversion of 'To be or not to be' from speech to mime robs Hamlet of another chance to communicate directly with his audience. (...)

At first the Tragedians seem to inhabit the same world as Rosencrantz and Guildenstern. They get involved in the absurd coin-spinning, complain that they have no control, and join in the empty speculation about chance and fate. With this 'existential' attitude goes an inverted form of theatre:

> We keep to our usual stuff, more or less, only inside out.
> We do on stage the things that are supposed to happen off.
> Which is a kind of integrity, if you look on every
> exit being an entrance somewhere else.

They are prepared to portray *flagrante delicto* and they even countenance audience participation. All this goes under the title of realism. And since Rosencrantz and Guildenstern too are doing on stage the things that are supposed to happen off—in *Hamlet*—this passage provides another reason for considering them as 'real' characters. But soon the Tragedians' style changes. Guildenstern persuades them to present an orthodox play rather than one of their inverted 'performances', and the Player seems suddenly to change from a 'real' person to an actor, 'Always in character', like the *Hamlet* cast. This association with *Hamlet* is immediately cemented when, in place of the expected play by the Tragedians, Stoppard gives us a scene from *Hamlet*. It is as if the Tragedians have been somehow metamorphosed into the cast of *Hamlet*. (...)

I hope it is clear from this account that the Tragedians do not do what we might reasonably have expected them to do; they do not shuttle back and forth between the 'mystery' and the 'clockwork' in order to provide common ground for the 'real' characters of Rosencrantz and Guildenstern and the 'artificial' characters of Hamlet and company throughout the play. Instead, they make one decisive shift, late in Act I, from the 'real' to the 'artificial'. Thus they are never really in a position to mediate between the two worlds, and the play is consequently less dramatic than it might have been. Nevertheless, the Tragedians do serve a number of useful purposes. Firstly, their abandonment of the world of Rosencrantz and Guildenstern underscores the intensifying sense of isolation which the pair feel as the play proceeds. It should be noted that the full effect of the change in the Tragedians is not felt until the middle of Act II, which is when Guildenstern is becoming particularly anxious about the other problems which I have defined. Secondly, by removing the Tragedians from the 'real' world of Rosencrantz and Guildenstern Stoppard has not completely deprived himself of a link between this world and the 'clockwork' world which the Tragedians now inhabit alongside the cast of *Hamlet*. For although there is now a *psychological* rift between the Tragedians and the protagonists, the two groups continue to encounter each other *physically*, so that, on this level at least, there persists a sense of drama rather than sheer juxtaposition. In fact one of the main functions of the Tragedians is to develop the abstract antithesis between the world of *Hamlet* and the world of Rosencrantz and Guildenstern into a physical confrontation full of fear and menace. In Acts II and III the Tragedians act as surrogates for the *Hamlet* cast—surrogates who, because of their freedom from a pre-existing Shakespearean text, can activate or dramatize the clash between the two worlds. This sense of physical menace first becomes strong just prior to 'The Mousetrap' rehearsal. The confrontation between Rosencrantz and the Player here is a replay of their Act I confrontation, but this time the Player rather than Rosencrantz comes off best, and Rosencrantz emerges hurt and frightened. What follows is even more alarming:

> *He makes a break for an exit.* A TRAGEDIAN *dressed as a* KING *enters.* ROS *recoils, breaks for the opposite wing. Two cloaked* TRAGEDIANS *enter.* ROS *tries again but another* TRAGEDI-AN *enters, and* ROS *retires to midstage.*

This note of menace is maintained during the rehearsal, particularly at its climax: the death of the two spies, who are stage replicas of Rosencrantz and Guildenstern. At this point Rosencrantz and Guildenstern are only half-aware of the resemblance between them and the spies and therefore of the threat posed to them by the spies' deaths; but the replay of these deaths in Act III finally convinces them that they are doomed. The context of this replay, incidentally, provides a good example of the way in which Stoppard uses the Tragedians to flesh out the threats posed to Rosencrantz and Guildenstern by the *Hamlet* plot: Rosencrantz and Guildenstern read the death-warrant which Hamlet has prepared for them, and immediately they are threatened physically by the Tragedians:

> *One by one the* PLAYERS *emerge, impossibly, from the barrel, and form a casually menacing circle round* ROS *and* GUIL *who are still appalled and mesmerized.*

The impossibility of this appearance of six people from a single barrel draws attention to the unreal clockwork nature of the Tragedians' world.

So Stoppard uses the Tragedians in *Rosencrantz and Guildenstern Are Dead* to make tangible the forces threatening his protagonists in order to provide a modicum of action in a play which deals largely with the inner man. But a much more important function of the Tragedians is to elucidate the basic clash between the real and the artificial on which the play depends. This task of elucidation begins almost as soon as the Tragedians appear at Claudius's court in Act II. In the midst of his plangent account of the spectatorless performance given in response to Guildenstern's commission in Act I the Player lets slip a crucial definition: 'We're *actors*—we're the opposite of people!' At this point it is the Player who seems to be out of his element, but it very soon becomes apparent that in the world of *Hamlet* it is the 'actors' who are at home and the 'real' people like Rosencrantz and Guildenstern who are lost. Later in Act II this point emerges clearly from an exchange (modelled on a passage early in James Saunders' *Next Time I'll Sing to You*) between Guildenstern and the Player:

> GUIL: But we don't know what's going on, or what to do with ourselves. We don't know how to act.
> PLAYER: Act natural ...

The emphasis on the word 'act' in Guildenstern's speech indicates that Stoppard is still using it in its technical sense; he is maintaining the dichotomy between people and actors. The Player now proceeds to define the kind of world that actors inhabit:

There's a design at work in all art—surely you know that? Events must play themselves out to aesthetic, moral and logical conclusion [*sic*] ... we aim at the point where everyone who is marked for death dies.... It is *written* ... We follow directions—there is no *choice* involved. The bad end unhappily, the good unluckily. That is what tragedy means.[1]

This world, unlike the 'real' world of Rosencrantz and Guildenstern, has form and meaning, and death is an accepted part of its design. To be sure, for the Tragedians, as for Rosencrantz and Guildenstern, 'there is no *choice* involved', but in the case of the Tragedians there is a transparent logic behind this lack of choice, and anyway, the death that is ordained for them is only a mock death:

Do you know what happens to old actors? ...
Nothing. They're still acting.

Guildenstern reacts with derision to this ordered, artificial view of the world, especially to its stylized version of death:

Actors! The mechanics of cheap melodrama! That isn't *death*! ... You scream and choke and sink to your knees, but it doesn't bring death home to anyone—it doesn't catch them unawares and start the whisper in their skulls that says—'One day you are going to die.' ...

This verbal disagreement is bolstered visually by the confrontation between the 'real' Rosencrantz and Guildenstern and their replicas, and particularly by the contrast, here and at the end of Act III, between the 'dramatic' death acted out by the spies and the 'real' death defined by Guildenstern.

NOTE

1. The Player is, of course, echoing Wilde's Miss Prism, who defines fiction in similar terms early in Act II of *The Importance of Being Earnest*. This is perhaps the point at which to observe that Wilde too was fascinated by Rosencrantz and Guildenstern. Clearly Stoppard's debt to Wilde extends beyond *Travesties*.

—Richard Corballis, *Stoppard, the Mystery and the Clockwork*, (New York: Methuen, 1984): pp. 35–36, 42–43, 44–47.

[Neil Sammells, the Dean of Humanities at Bath Spa University, has published *Wilde Style: The Plays and Prose of Oscar Wilde*. Here, he discusses the conflicting views of art held by Guildenstern and the Player as they relate to the theater as a metaphor for life].

In Stoppard's play the problems resurface in Guildenstern's encounter with *Hamlet*. His responses to the action which sweeps in from the wings argue his search for a significance in events to justify the pattern of art, proclaiming *order* as *meaning*. In the Player, of course, he meets a suitable opponent. Truth, claims the Player, is just the currency of living: 'There may be nothing behind it, but it doesn't make any difference so long as it is honoured' (p. 48). Guildenstern yearns for *meaning*, while the Player will settle for *order*, calmly relinquishing control if that is what is required. (...)

'There's a design at work in all art—surely you know that?' the Player says to Guildenstern, 'Events must play themselves out to aesthetic, moral and logical conclusion' (p. 57). Art is remorseless in its demands: 'we aim,' he continues, icily, 'at the point where everyone who is marked for death dies' (p. 57). The art of the Player's life is the murderous relish with which he obeys the dictates of this sensationally familiar world. Guildenstern's quarrel with him is about the nature of the design which is in art. In mirroring life it must reveal meaning and significance, not just impose its own shape. When the players enact a theatrical slaughter Guildenstern can discern no truth in their cheap melodrama; 'it doesn't catch them unawares,' he says of a potential audience, 'and start the whisper in their skulls that says——"One day you are going to die"' (p. 61). He plunges a toy dagger into the Player and, along with Stoppard's audience, is fooled by the mechanics of cheap melodrama. After a brief silence the tragedians applaud as the Player stands and brushes himself down. In upholding the rights of life against the deformations of cheap art, in attempting to get the actor to come to grips with life at least once, by killing him, Guildenstern unwittingly demonstrates the fictional nature of what he conceives to be the real.

In asking what drama really is, in following the metadramatic strategies of *Next Time I'll Sing To You*, *Rosencrantz and Guildenstern Are Dead* conducts a similar investigation into the notion of theatre as a metaphor for life. This preoccupation links the related concerns with the problem of identity and the nature of art. By turning *Hamlet* upside down Stoppard asks whether tragedy is an adequate metaphor for the way we live our lives. It is Guildenstern who says, as we have already seen, 'All your life you live so close to truth, it becomes a permanent blur in the corner of your eye, and when something nudges it into outline it is like being ambushed by a grotesque' (p. 28). Stoppard 'defamiliarises' *Hamlet*; he performs a critical function which nudges it into new and unfamiliar outline.

On a more complex level, Stoppard explores the theatre–life metaphor by examining the related roles of critic and artist. Guildenstern's personality is defined by his relationship to *Hamlet*, by his fluctuation (and here we can see a parallel with Stoppard's description of the plight of the Beckettian refugee) between his earnest desire to make sense of, to criticise, the action around him, and his occasional capitulation to a design he accepts but does not understand. 'To be taken in hand and led,' he says, sacrificing the struggle for freedom for the comforts of compulsion, 'like being a child again.... It's like being given a prize, an extra slice of childhood when you least expect it' (p. 29). 'One of the reasons that the play turned out to work so well, I think,' said Stoppard in a television interview, 'is that the predicament of the characters coincides with the predicament of the playwright.' In fact, in *Rosencrantz and Guildenstern Are Dead*, Stoppard handles his predicament rather more successfully than his two main characters: by turning the stone upside down, to see what it looks like the wrong way up, Stoppard demonstrates that initiative which Guildenstern denies. By criticising *Hamlet*, in effect, Stoppard disrupts the internal power-structure of the work, elevating to a position of unwonted dominance the play's own continual questioning of the nature of art, its own thoroughgoing awareness of the degree to which life and action are conditioned by the forms we have adopted to make it comprehensible. Stoppard succeeds where Guildenstern fails; he does not act *in* Shakespeare's drama, he acts *upon* it.

—Neil Sammells, *Tom Stoppard: The Artist as Critic*, (New York: St. Martin's, 1988): pp. 37–38.

Jumpers

On one level, *Jumpers* is a showy, theatrical murder mystery that's never solved. On another level, it is a serious investigation of philosophical principles.

Act One opens with a party at the Moores' flat. Offstage, Archie introduces Dorothy "Dotty" Moore, a musical comedy actress (now retired) and the party's hostess. She begins to sing, "Shine on Harvest Moon," but breaks off quickly upon realizing the lyrics are not right. In the background, the Secretary is swinging in and out of the spotlight and covers the entire stage's distance from end-to-end. With each re-appearance, she is wearing fewer clothes until she is naked and knocks over Crouch and his serving tray of drinks.

Archie introduces the yellow-clad Jumpers with much fanfare, but they only are ragtag gymnasts, to Dotty's disappointment. The Jumpers arrange themselves into a human pyramid, a gunshot goes off and a Jumper falls out of the pyramid. Dotty walks through the gap. The injured Jumper grabs Dotty's legs and tries to pull himself up, in the process rubbing his bloody body on her white dress. The rest of the pyramid collapses and Dorothy screams for Archie. Archie, still offstage, tells everyone that the party is over and counsels Dotty to keep the Jumper hidden until morning.

Dotty watches a special on TV about a moon landing. The lunar commander kicks his subordinate off the ladder leading up their crippled space capsule, stranding the second man on the moon. Dotty is enraptured, still in the same position and holding the Jumper, who is now dead.

In the study, the Secretary walks in to take dictation from George, a Professor of Moral Philosophy, who is preparing notes for a lecture on "Man: good, bad, or indifferent?" Dotty impotently cries for help but is unheard as George ramblingly ponders the question, "is God?" out loud. His musings are punctuated by Dotty screaming, "Murder—Rape—Wolves!" George finally hears her screams and yells at her to quiet down.

He continues with a discourse on the God of Goodness and the God of Creation; he has taken up a bow and arrow and mentions Zeno the philosopher, who theorized that an arrow shot covers half the distance to its target, then half the remaining distance, ad infinitum, never reaching its target. At that moment, Dotty screams "Fire!" and George accidentally looses the arrow. It sails over the wardrobe, clearly refuting Zeno. George continues to ponder his lecture then wanders into the bedroom, looking for his hare Thumper. He sees but ignores Dotty, who is lying facedown and naked on the bed. Dotty pleads with George to stay with her. He never notices the dead Jumper hidden in the bedroom. George is more interested in talking about his lecture and Dotty admonishes him for "living in dreamland."

She is exasperated with George and says that she wants Archie to visit her again. George is suspicious of the frequency of Archie's visits and the fact that Dottie receives him in her bedroom. Dotty wants understanding and help; she's not getting it from George, so she turns to Archie, a doctor who keeps her spirits up. George hasn't noticed that Dotty is having psychological troubles again.

George reminisces about the first day he met Dotty, when he was a professor and she a student in his class. Dotty tries to tell George that she's in trouble and needs his help. She is exasperated with him, asking, "Haven't you invented God *yet*?" (p. 19). They're interrupted by the sound of jets, signaling a parade in celebration of the Radical Liberal Party victory. Dotty repeats Archie's opinions of politics.

Dotty takes a goldfish bowl into the bathroom and reemerges with the bowl on her head, imitating a moonwalker. She informs George that the church will be "rationalized" by Sam Clegthorpe, the Radical Liberal spokesman—and agnostic scientist—who is the new Archbishop of Canterbury. Dotty recounts what stopped her career: singing about the romantic moon was somehow spoiled by images of gray-clad moonwalkers with goldfish bowls on their heads on TV. George continues to ponder science versus God.

"Good" and "bad" are merely our perceptions of something, says Dotty, quoting Archie's moral relativism. She lapses into song titles about a romantic moon, breaking into sobs as George holds her, playing with her hair until he asks if she's seen his rabbit Thumper. He leaves to go to the study and Dotty puts the corpse in a chair. George looks for his tortoise Pat in the bedroom and Dotty uses her robe to conceal the Jumper's body from George's view. He picks up the bow and arrow when the doorbell rings, assuming it's Archie.

Upon opening the front door, he finds that the visitor is Inspector Bones holding some flowers, asking to see Dotty. The blustery Inspector says that the law is black-and-white. If the phone call that brought him to the flat is in error, he says he'd like to meet Dotty, an actress he admires. If she's guilty, he declares, the law will show no mercy.

The Inspector starts towards the living room when George reveals that he was the anonymous caller, pretending to be a neighbor calling about the noisy party. The party was a Rad-Lib celebratory party, also attended by Professor Duncan McFee, a Professor of Logic—George's academic adversary—who believes that notions of "good" and "bad" are only normative social rules for living, not moral absolutes.

George tells Dotty he's willing to take the blame (for the party-noise phone call) and she misunderstands, thinking he'll take responsibility for the murder. The Inspector asks if McFee is a part-time acrobat and George affirms. Bones starts to think the whole situation is crazy and goes to meet Dotty. He is awestruck by the sight of Dotty and they stare at each other as if frozen. The Jumper's body crashes to the floor, unheard.

Archie comes in through the front door, elegantly dressed. He lets seven Jumpers in the front door, carrying what looks to be a TV camera and lighting equipment. Archie opens a small bit of material, unwrapping it until it is a large plastic bag. The Jumpers throw the body into the bag and carry it out the front door.

At the beginning of Act Two, Bones thinks that Dotty committed the murder and wants to get a psychiatric witness that will keep her out of jail. George, still confused, thinks that he's talking about the noise complaint, and Bones thinks he's protecting Dotty. When told there is a dead body, George thinks Bones has gone crazy.

Archie gives the Inspector his business card, listing "Sir Archibald Jumper" as a "doctor of medicine, philosophy, literature and law, with diplomas in psychological medicine and P.T. including gym." When Archie mentions that his trampoline team has an opening, Bones asks what's happened to Professor McFee, to which Archie replies that McFee is dead and he, Archie, is to blame. Bones doesn't believe him. Archie fends off Bones' attempt to question Dotty by saying she is his patient.

Archie tries to convince Bones that McFee was depressed and shot himself in a large plastic bag. He produces a suicide note and coroner's certificate as confirmation. While Bones considers the matter, Archie offers him the Chair of Divinity, then the Chair of Logic when they are interrupted by Dotty's cry of "MURDER!"

George returns to his lecture and mentions G. E. Moore, an absolutist philosopher. George says, "there is more in me than meets the microscope" as he and Archie discuss the atheism versus belief in God. Archie tells George that McFee is dead and George wanders onto the notion that "atheism [is] a sort of crutch for those who can't bear the reality of God."

Dotty yells, "Rape!" and they enter the bedroom and see Bones standing above Dotty, who is sobbing on the bed. Bones says that he didn't touch her and Archie sees an opportunity to arrange a deal. Bones leaves.

Now that the Chair of Logic is vacant because of McFee's murder, George requests to Archie that he be appointed to the position. George discovers the dead goldfish in the bathroom and screams at Dotty. Crouch comes in the front door and implies to George that Dotty killed McFee. George says, mistakenly, that Dotty and Archie are eating McFee in the casserole.

Crouch admits he also anonymously called the police about the murder. George sees that the curtains are drawn around the bed and Archie and Dotty have a TV camera and lighting set up, supposedly attributable to the dermatograph, which analyzes the skin's surface. Crouch tells Archie that McFee was his friend and that the Secretary was McFee's mistress; she was secretly engaged to him but didn't know he was married. Further, McFee told her it was over and he intended to go into a monastery. Archie tells

Crouch that it is not certain who killed McFee, that life isn't a murder mystery. The Secretary puts on her white coat, which has a blood stain on it, but which is explained when George goes to the cupboard and sees his rabbit Thumper, impaled with an arrow (and it was he who shot the hare). He steps back and crushes his turtle Pat. He yells, "'Dotty! Help! Murder!'" as the screen shows erotic close-ups of Dotty's skin.

In the closing Coda, the Symposium takes place in dream form and Crouch presides as Chairman and is attended by Jumpers in yellow gowns. The first to speak on the subject of "Man—good, bad or indifferent?" is Sir Archibald Jumper, who speaks in jibberish. The Jumpers hold up favorable scores on scorecards. Next is Captain Horatio Scott, the astronaut who left his fellow astronaut on the moon. George doesn't speak, but the Archbishop of Canterbury (Clegthorpe) is called in his place and refuses to take the oath because he doubts God's existence. After some interrogation, Archie yells, *Will no one rid me of this turbulent priest* (first edition)/*copper's nark* (second edition)?" The Jumpers arrange themselves and Clegthorpe into a pyramid, as in the beginning of the play. Clegthorpe is shot and is knocked out of the pyramid, which falls apart. Dotty is called next and she sings "Sentimental Journey." George screams *"Stop!!"* As everything freezes, he talks about intelligent people pondering God and that life is good and better than death. Archie says that everything works out and Dotty ends by saying, "Goodbye spoony Juney Moon."

Jumpers

George Moore, a 40-to-50-year-old attractive man, shares his name with philosopher G. E. Moore. He holds the Chair of Moral Philosophy, a low-ranking chair at the University. He lets his thinking get in the way of his actions or feelings. As Dotty accuses, he is a dreamer. He eventually reasons his way into moral absolutes and God as he prepares for giving a lecture on the subject of "Man: Good, bad or indifferent?" As he philosophizes, he fails to notice that his wife is hiding a dead body in her bedroom. Even though he suspects his wife is having an affair with Archie, he is unable to get emotionally closer to her. In any case, he's suspicious of Archie and perhaps somewhat jealous of him as well. The only real remorse he shows is for the death of his pet hare and tortoise at his own hands, even though he did nothing to stop Clegthorpe from being shot in the Coda.

Dorothy "Dotty" Moore, George's significantly younger wife—and as her name suggests—is a warm, sensual and stunning ex-musical comedy singer/actress who now mixes up the lyrics of idealized songs about the moon. Her disillusionment came as the people who landed on the moon wrecked her idea of romanticism. Her marriage to George is far from intimate, although she does try to reach out to him on numerous occasions. It's clear that some of the romance has worn off since she met George as a student in his class. She may be having an affair with Archie (or not) and repeats many of the opinions he gives her. Archie, at least, helps her take care of the "problem" of the murdered Jumper.

Sir Archibald Jumper or "Archie" is a well-rounded Renaissance man and a "dandy" as old as or older than George. In addition to holding a variety of degrees and titles ranging from doctor of medicine to a diploma in gym, he is also the Vice-Chancellor of the University, making him George's boss. In contrast with George, Archie is a man of action. Morally, he is a relativist or a Logical-Positivist; as such, he is the leader of the yellow-clad Jumpers. In his eyes, murder is not morally wrong. He comes to Dotty's aid by disposing of the body of Duncan McFee. In this way, he is able to help her whereas George is not. His interest in Dotty may be more than medical and they may be having an affair.

Inspector Bones is a middle-aged, carelessly-dressed inspector and an absolutist in the way he sees the law as being black and white. On the tip from an anonymous caller, he shows up at the Moores' flat to investigate a murder. He has a love of musical comedies, though, and is an ardent admirer of Miss Dorothy Moore. When he intuits that she may have committed the murder, he immediately changes his philosophy and tries to think of ways to clear her name legally. His career may ultimately be discredited by Archie, who finds him in Dotty's bedroom after she screams "Rape!"

Duncan McFee is George's professional rival and the Chair of Logic. He was performing with the Jumpers at the Moores' party when he was shot and killed; it is his body that is the subject of debate and inquiry in the events after the party. Although he was once a staunch supporter of the Logical-Positivists, it is brought to light after his death that he had changed his views to that of moral absolutism. He was married; before his death, he was going to break off his affair with George's secretary and enter a monastery.

Crouch is a small, old porter, who is, as his name would suggest, crouched. He was pressed into serving drinks at the Moore's party, where he is knocked over by the stripping-secretary-on-a-swing. He had befriended and learned some philosophical principles from Duncan McFee; it is he who holds vital information about McFee's affair and his plan to enter a monastery. He chairs the dream symposium in the Coda.

The Secretary is a silent presence throughout the proceedings. Young, attractive and obviously sensual, as her striptease on the swing suggests, she takes George's dictation for his lecture notes. She is poker-faced and discreet—she had an affair with and was secretly engaged to Duncan McFee.

Sam Clegthorpe, the newly-appointed Archbishop of Canterbury, was formerly the Radical Liberal spokesman for Agriculture, as well as a scientist and agnostic. He is killed in the Coda, shot out of the Jumpers' pyramid like McFee. His appeal to George for help right before his death went unheeded.

Captain Horatio Scott saved himself by pushing his subordinate, Astronaut Oates, off the ladder leading to their crippled space capsule. He was able to return to Earth while Oates was left behind on the moon.

The Jumpers are a group of Radical Liberals whose ragtag gymnastics feats are underwhelming. They wear identical yellow uniforms and aren't as necessarily young or athletic as one would assume such "jumpers" to be.

Jumpers

G. B. CRUMP ON GEORGE'S FAILURES

[G. B. Crump, who teaches at Central Missouri State University and has published studies of R. M. Koster and Wright Morris, argues that although George is able to think and reason, he is unable to act, which leads to his shortcomings as a husband and a detective.]

These details favorable to George are undercut by others which suggest that he fails as a husband and as a detective. The nature of the failure is implied in Stoppard's choice of G. E. Moore as a model for his hero. Although respected as a philosopher, Moore was notorious among his acquaintances for what one writer calls "an almost childlike naiveté concerning ordinary affairs."[16] In *Russell and Moore*, A. J. Ayer quotes J. M. Keynes on Moore's "unworldliness and his indifference to the 'qualities of a life of action'" (p. 137) and points out that Moore himself conceded that his work took its "main stimulus" not "from direct reflection on the world or the sciences but rather from what other philosophers had said about them" (p. 141). All these traits are displayed by the George of *Jumpers*. The self-reflexive nature of his thought is represented by his lecturing before a mirror; he is talking only to himself. The opening stage directions stipulate that either Dorothy's bedroom (which looks out on the world through French windows and television) or George's study must be blacked out, thereby dramatizing the radical separation between the abstract conceptual world of his philosophizing and the "real" world of her breakdown and McFee's corpse. Because of his isolation, George consistently learns of developments in the public drama of the radical-liberal coup and the private drama of the murder indirectly, through others.

George's love for the rarefied atmosphere of abstract logic results in a destructive indifference to human concerns. He dismisses political events as insignificant, yet they have great influence on the actual lives of people. In the *Coda*, he is unwilling or unable to defend the new Archbishop of Canterbury, who, like Thomas à Becket, faces martyrdom when he begins to take his role as spiritual leader seriously. In view of Dorothy's special role in the play, the fact that George is her husband rather than a mere lover like Bones or Archie suggests that he has a closer relationship to "reality" and ought to better comprehend the trauma she suffers. But George repeatedly fails Dorothy as a husband. When she cries first "Murder!" and then "Rape!" Bones and Archie go to her aid, but George disregards her cries for help, responding only when they get so loud that they disrupt his train of thought. In the larger sense, he overlooks her crisis of unbelief: "*Please don't leave me!* I don't want to be left, to cope" (p. 41), Dorothy begs him (almost as if George himself were God), but belief in God is for him a philosophical issue, not a pressing human need. When Dorothy promises to stop seeing Archie and weeps on George's breast, his heart is described in the stage directions as "*uncomprehending*" (p. 41), and he returns to his study rejecting her invitation. George's eloquence in the *Coda* is unable to restore Dorothy's lost sense of romance; and the play ends with her farewell to the "spoony Juney moon" (p. 87), a symbol for the ideal of undying marital love and fidelity. This gesture suggests that she will turn from her husband to her lover. George's indifference helps to destroy his marriage and, by extension, the civilizing forces of moral tradition and social stability that the institution of marriage embodies.

In the instance of George, philosophy has degenerated into sterile academic debate divorced from the issues actually troubling man. For this reason, he cannot fill Dorothy's need for spiritual assurances, and she must perforce turn to Archie, who can at least help in disposing of the corpse. George's misordering of human priorities is epitomized by the fact that he is more worried about Thumper and Pat, the rabbit and tortoise he uses to refute Zeno's paradoxes, than about Dorothy and McFee.

As a detective, George is no more astute than Bones. He is the last person in the play to learn there has been a murder, his ignorance continuing through several scenes in which others discuss the killing with him but he misunderstands because of various linguistic confusions: for George as for Bones, language is a trap. At one point, he accepts Archie's improbable suicide story. George's eventual solution to the murder is cast in the same language and issues from the same arbitrary intuitive leap as his conclusions about God: "There are many things I know which are not verifiable but nobody can tell me I don't know them, and I think that I know that something happened to poor Dotty and she somehow killed McFee, as sure as she killed my poor Thumper" (p. 78). The last part of this deduction undercuts the reliability of George's overall solution, for the audience eventually learns that George himself shot the rabbit by accident when he mistook Dorothy's cry of "fire" (a noun) for a command to fire (imperative verb) his bow and arrow.

Going to answer the door and expecting to greet Archie, George says to his turtle, "Now might I do it, Pat" (p. 43). The line echoes that of Hamlet as he passes up his chance to stab the praying Claudius. Like Hamlet, George is guilty of thinking too much, and because he is so absorbed in resolving issues solely on the conceptual plane, he is never able to dispatch his rival Archie and regain Dorothy's affections. When George discovers Thumper impaled on his arrow, he utters his own cry for help, for the emotional support he has denied Dorothy. Though a final humanizing touch, that cry once more emphasizes George's ineffectuality in the realm of action.

NOTE

16. John O. Nelson, "Moore, George Edward," *Encyclopedia of Philosophy*, 1967 ed., p. 373.

> —G. B. Crump, "The Universe as Murder Mystery: Tom Stoppard's *Jumpers*," *Contemporary Literature* 20, 3 (1979): pp. 366–368.

Lucina Paquet Gabbard on the Symbolism of the Characters

[In this excerpt, Gabbard explains that the characters represent institutions or facets of society that try to solve the mystery of man, including morality, politics, escapism, and justice.]

A twist of the kaleidoscope and all these private characters assume an almost allegorical significance. Each becomes a symbol of some segment of society or some institution aimed at righting the world and solving the mystery of man's presence on this planet. George is the upholder of belief in God and the morality of man, but his developing deterioration represents their precarious position. As George explains, the burden of proof passed from atheists to believers. This tenuous state is magnified when George, elevated to symbolic level, becomes the universal representative of theology and ethics. This pedantic little man stands alone against the swollen tide of Jumpers who, George says, are chiefly logical positivists "with a linguistic analyst or two, a couple of Benthamite Utilitarians ... lapsed Kantians and empiricists generally ... and of course the usual Behaviourists" (pp. 50–51). George further erodes God's position through his language. By George's semantic twists, God becomes a "theological soubriquet" for the "first Cause" (p. 27); or, as the "first term of the series," George explains that "God, so to speak, is nought" (p. 29). At the height of his frustrations George cries:

> How does one know what it is one believes when it is so diffi-
> cult to know what it is one knows. I don't claim to know that
> God exists, I only claim that He does without my knowing it,
> and while I claim as much I do not claim to know as much;
> indeed I cannot know and God knows I cannot. (p. 71)

However despondent, George's words ring with atrophying heroism alongside Dotty's wonder at the universal automatic appeal to a god whom everyone insists is dead (p. 35).

Morality suffers from the same confusion. George is the solitary spokesman for moral absolutes; he believes that philosophers who view goodness as relative live in moral limbo. He cites language as a principal cause of this moral confusion. George says that every year the symposium's subject is "Man—good, bad, or indifferent?"; but enough disagreement about its meaning is always generated to ensure a change in the discussions (p. 46). Unfortunately, George's egocentric and unfeeling reactions to Dotty indicate that his own morality is smothered by pedantry. At the end of Act II, theology and ethics seem bereft of this last defender. George discovers that he, not

Dotty, has killed Thumper—with an arrow shot to prove God's existence. In the shock of realizing himself a killer, George steps backward, and "CRRRRRUNCH!!!" he kills his tortoise. His sobs blend into the Coda where he lies prostrate in the grip of a bizarre dream.

Even in George's dream, Archie is in charge. Symbolically, Archie is leadership—the repository of man's hopes and abdicated responsibilities. And Archie has led all segments of society down the path of expediency and amorality. Archie's intellectuals—education—are corrupt and ineffective, jumping from one pose to another at Archie's convenience and command. According to George, they are all as mad as McFee, who thinks lying and murder are merely anti-social, not inherently wrong. The general acceptance of such beliefs is witnessed by their philosophical classification—"Orthodox mainstream" (p. 49). The ineptitude of all these thinkers is exposed when Archie reveals the basis of their selection. For the new chairman of the Philosophy Department, he wants a man of good standing who need not know much philosophy.

As leader of the Radical Liberals, winners of the recent election, Archie also represents politics. But like morality, democracy depends on perception: it is all in the head, Archie has told Dottie. When George protests, Dotty retorts: "It's not the voting that's democracy, it's the counting" (p. 35). Language plays its tricks again. As a result of this "election," the Church Commissioners were dispossessed, the Newspaper Proprietors found themselves in a police car, Clegthorpe—agricultural spokesman and agnostic—has been appointed Archbishop of Canterbury, and early next week the Police Force will become only a ceremonial front. The image of the failure of politics is intensified in the first scene when the whole pyramid of Rad-Lib Jumpers has been seen to collapse under the removal of logic— the death of McFee. In the Coda, the pyramid is rebuilt with Archbishop Clegthorpe, "The highpoint of scientism" (p. 39), as its pinnacle. But once more a gunshot—violence—intervenes. Clegthorpe is toppled, and the pyramid disintegrates.

Dotty, of course, stands for escapism. She is sex, show business, and romance rolled into one. Her songs about Juney moons, her millions of undaunted admirers, her flirtations and infidelities speak of man's fantasies. But this symbol too has collapsed. Dotty faltered in the middle of her act and addressed herself to the mystery of another absolute: "why must the damned show go on anyway?" (p. 39).

Summoned by fearful anonymity is Bones—symbol of law, order, and justice. He is supposed to be even-handed and incorruptible—able to detect the evil-doers and empowered to right their wrongs by punishment. However, Bones, the implacable law, is also human. Victimized by Dotty's charms, Bones instructs Archie to temper justice with romantic illusion, dirty tricks, and prejudice; with Dotty in the witness box, he thinks the battle will be half won. The other half, he says, will require getting something on Mad Jock McFee. Finally, made vulnerable by his fantasies, Bones, the full majesty of the law, is frightened into retreat by Dotty's blackmail. But the mystery remains: who killed McFee? And the criminal is still at large.

The secretary and Crouch, of course, represent the mute, lowly ones who only watch and serve. But they are victims too. Stripping on the flying trapeze, the secretary concretizes man swinging between the darknesses of ignorance and false hopes, from the innocence of the womb to the reality of the tomb. The moments of light in between represent those flashes of insight which strip him, little by little, of his beliefs and illusions. Crouch, representing the servile ones, is so blinded by his workaday world that he doubts neither his own inferiority, nor the Jumpers' expertise. Unseeing, he backs into the swing's path and gets knocked "arse over tip" by the nude lady (p. 18). He never knows what has hit him until he is blacked out in the crash. But in the Coda, Crouch has become Chairman of the Symposium.

Catalysts to it all, the moon men are science and technology raised to the ultimate power. The scientific method was intended to provide the objectivity that would unlock the secrets of the universe. Instead it unloosed an invasion by machines— television cameras exploring the surface of the moon and the skin of Dotty's body. It unloosed astronauts in gold fish bowls landing their amorality on the moon. In the Coda, Archie puts rationalizations into Captain Scott's mouth. He orders Scott to explain his "instinctive considerations" in relation to his seniority over Oates, their respective importance to the world, and his responsibility to himself. Scott has only to answer, "That's it" (p. 84). The spectacle of these astronauts fighting on the moon caused McFee to doubt himself. Perhaps the most far-reaching effect was on Dotty: for her it was all over once man gazed down from the moon and saw earth "little-local" with all its absolutes looking "like the local customs of another place" (pp. 74–75).

> —Lucina Paquet Gabbard, *The Stoppard Plays*, (Troy, N.Y.: Whitston Pub. Co., 1982): pp. 92–95.

RICHARD CORBALLIS ON ARCHIE VERSUS GEORGE

[Here Corballis compares and contrasts the views of Archie and George in the play and concludes that the play supports George's faith in intuition].

Sir Archibald Jumper, M.D., D.Phil., D.Litt., L.D., D.P.M., D.P.T. (Gym.), embodies the spirit of the Radical Liberal Party which has just come to power in a general election. The Party is dedicated to rationalism, or scientism as George calls it. This attitude is epitomized by their plan to rationalize the Church. Already the Radical Liberal spokesman for Agriculture has been made Archbishop of Canterbury and an unspecified building containing magnificent stained glass has been converted into a gymnasium. Archie himself, as his qualifications suggest, is something of a Renaissance Man; he has expertise in an impossibly wide range of fields that has been acquired by dedication to rational inquiry. This same dedication causes him and his colleagues to associate themselves with classical Greece and with 'the Athens of the North', Edinburgh. Archie's dedication to reason has led him, like A. J. Ayer, whom some regard as his real-life prototype, to embrace an extreme form of positivism. (...)

Archie is capable of defending his position in glib and

plausible terms but the play is at pains to point out that, at best, his interpretation of things is only skin-deep, like the superficial posturings of the Jumpers, and that, at worst—and this is what makes him a more disturbing character than Lord Malquist— this lack of depth can lead to tyranny after the manner of Henry II and Richard III or Hitler, Stalin or Nero or sundry military dictators of recent times.

Archie's shallowness is indicated in all sorts of ways, for instance by the fact that he needs only two minutes to prepare a philosophical paper. But it is the introduction of the dermatograph which demonstrates most forcibly that his scientism is, quite literally, only skin-deep. (...)

The contrast between Archie's 'clockwork' aloofness and George's full-blooded sensuality is reflected on a more abstract plane in the contrast between Archie's scientism and George's faith in intuition, which leads him to insist that 'there is more in me than meets the microscope'. Like Professor Anderson in *Professional Foul*, with whom he also shares an interest in sport, a respect for instincts, and a conviction that rights are different from rules, George is better at criticizing the principles of his antagonists than at proving his own case. He establishes easily that 'if rationality were the criterion for things being allowed to exist, the world would be one gigantic field of soya beans', and again that Archie's positivism makes 'one man's idea of good ... no more meaningful than another man's whether he be St Francis or ...'—and it is Archie himself who completes the state-ment—'Hitler or Stalin or Nero'. But when it comes to establishing the existence of God or the validity of the proposition that 'Good and evil are metaphysical absolutes', George runs into all sorts of difficulties, both in theory (witness his ridiculous attempts to dictate a lecture on these topics at the beginning of Act I) and in practice (witness the apparent failure of providence which allows George unwittingly to kill his hare and his tortoise in the course of the play). (...)

The net result of Crouch's intervention late in Act II is to warn the audience that Archie's triumph may not be as absolute as it seems. At the same time we may begin to see that George's collapse is less than total. Very early in the play George insures himself against the debilitating effect of his chronic linguistic ineptitude by insisting that there is a great difference between language and meaning and that confusion in the former does not necessarily signify confusion in the latter. The unfortunate deaths of his pets do not scupper George's religious instincts either, since he makes it clear that the God he acknowledges is not the naively providential God of religious observance. Moreover, long before he steps on Pat (the tortoise) George has contemplated the case of a man who accidentally crushes a beetle and has succeeded in extracting moral significance from the event. And the killing of Thumper (the hare), while it is distressing, does have a positive aspect: it demonstrates the point, which is an integral part of George's proof of the existence of God, that arrows do reach their targets, so that Saint Sebastian need not have died of fright.

And so as the Coda begins, the tension between Archie's scientism and George's intuitionism has still to be finally resolved. Technically this scene is a dream sequence devised by George's fevered imagination, and the depiction of events is certainly somewhat bizarre. But despite this dislocation in the mode of presentation there is no real discontinuity in either the themes or the characterization. It is particularly remarkable that there is no change in the portrayal of George; although the George of the Coda is his own projection of himself he remains the same old impractical figure, who refuses to intervene to save Clegthorpe from death. As far as the ideas are concerned, the Coda may be considered as a direct continuation of the preceding two acts.

For the most part the Coda is quite flippant in tone—too flippant perhaps to serve the purpose for which it seems to have been designed: to recommend George's views and discredit Archie's. The discrediting of Archie is effected by a number of factors, for example by Archie's own nonsense-speech in defence of scientism, by the way in which he manipulates Captain Scott's defence of his conduct on the moon (in the first edition only), and by Clegthorpe's betrayal of Archie, which re-enacts McFee's betrayal, as it was described by Crouch in Act II. The killing of Clegthorpe, with its echoes of Richard III's murder of Hastings and Henry II's disposal of Thomas à Becket, brings out Archie's tyrannical propensities, while the fact that the pyramid of Jumpers disintegrates as soon as Clegthorpe is shot out of it, instead of staying intact for a time as it did under similar conditions at the beginning of the play, seems to indicate that the morale of the Rad-Lib party is weakening. (...)

George (...)

at last (...)

manages to put together a defence of intuitionism which is as powerful and coherent as his big speech at the end of Act I. Even logical positivists, he contends,

> ... *know* that life is better than death, that love is better than hate, and that the light shining through the cast window of their bloody gymnasium is more beautiful than a rotting corpse.

But the last word goes to Archie. His curtain-speech is nothing if not ambiguous. The Bible rubs shoulders with Beckett,[1] and cynical undertones trouble the suave surface:

> Do not despair—many are happy much of the time; more eat than starve, more are healthy than sick, more curable than dying; not so many dying as dead; and one of the thieves was saved. Hell's bells and all's well—half the world is at peace with itself, and so is the other half; vast areas are unpolluted; millions of children grow up without suffering deprivation, and millions, while deprived, grow up without suffering cruelties, and millions, while deprived and cruelly treated, none the less grow up. No laughter is sad and many tears are joyful. At the graveside the undertaker doffs his hat and impregnates the prettiest mourner. Wham, bam, thank you Sam.

Still, even if Archie's final stance remains a shade obscure, it seems reasonable to conclude with Salmon that the play comes down on the side of George and the angels. Morally, if not in fact, 'mystery' has triumphed over 'clockwork' once again.

NOTE

1. The 'Sam' who is thanked at the end of the speech may be Samuel Beckett. Certainly Hayman believes that Stoppard found a way of saying thank-you to Beckett here. (The Sam could be Sam Clegthorpe, however, and anyway 'Wham, bam, thank you Sam' is a proverbial exclamation.) Stoppard himself, responding to Hayman's comment, talks of a parallelism at the end of *Jumpers*. But a parallelism is not the same thing as a thank-you and Stoppard may be referring to the Beckettian construction of Archie's speech, which continually gives with one hand and takes away with the other. Or perhaps the parallelism he has in mind is more specific: the Augustinian observation that 'one of the thieves was saved' is quoted in both *Godot* and *Murphy*, and in Stoppard's early story, 'Life, Times: Fragments'.

—Richard Corballis, *Stoppard, the Mystery and the Clockwork*, (New York: Methuen, 1984): pp. 64–65, 66–67, 73–74, 74–75, 76.

ANTHONY JENKINS ON DOTTY AND GEORGE'S EMOTIONAL SEPARATENESS

[Anthony Jenkins, formerly an Adjunct Professor of English at the University of Victoria and the writer of *Critical Essays on Tom Stoppard* and *Making of Victorian Drama*, notes that Dotty and George reach out to one another but ultimately fail each other. It is because of their lack of intimacy that Dotty seems to need Archie.]

Dotty and George's concern over absolute values is more than abstract word-play. Neither of them takes a moral stand, yet the ideas they give voice to have urgency because of Archie's manoeuvrings within the flat and the Rad-Libs' manipulations outside it and on the screen. But if *Jumpers* has darker undertones than any of its predecessors, it is also the first of Stoppard's works (apart from "Reunion") to explore a human relationship in any depth. The Malquists and the Moons, Constance and Alfred, Glad and Frank, Albert and Kate, even Ros and Guil for that matter, all talk past each other from within their self-absorbed enclosures. The Moores do that too, but they also make convincing attempts to reach each other, and the failure of those efforts creates a poignant, human drama at the centre of this verbal and theatrical whirligig. The fact that they are both intelligent people with a dry sense of their own inadequacies and absurdity gives them an unsentimental view of themselves and each other, but their intellect ultimately destroys their will. Dotty, shut away in her bedroom, takes refuge in her trauma when the going gets rough. George, buried in his notes or wandering purblind through the flat clutching his paraphernalia for his defence of love and goodness, takes cover amongst "matters of universal import" whenever demands are made on him. Yet the two do have moments of desolate or furious contact, and those episodes establish an ironic picture of two people who seem unable to put their well-meaning intuitions about universals into personal practice.

In the first of these episodes, the audience receive an immediate impression of a shared life from the way George can take Dotty's charade-playing for granted. Stoppard has frequently been accused of not understanding women or of failing to create a complex, believable female character, and Dotty has been singled out as the major weakness of *Jumpers*, but her behaviour here, though eccentric and stamped with her creator's own personality, has corners to it, facets and angles which make her a complicated, interesting and—given the play's established idiom—credible individual. All Stoppard's women characters have a sort of inner mysteriousness, an untouchable knowingness which makes them puzzling to their Moon-partners or provocative when allied with the worldly poise of a Harry (in pub or dental surgery), a Malquist or an Archie. Perhaps this impenetrability is the mark of what Stoppard cannot understand, but in *Jumpers* those hidden areas of personality make a dramatic impact. Dotty's external vibrance and neurotically destructive tendencies allow us to feel there is more to her than meets the eye, and Stoppard has given her moments with George in which we glimpse that inner self. In addition, he makes Dotty aware of her own mystery as a woman and a star—a mystery which she deliberately uses on George and later, quite lethally, on the Inspector.

Her first actions in the play as neurotic moon-singer, critic, and commander of the acrobats, or as a histrionic attention-seeker (with a penchant for Shakespeare) and player of ambiguous charades all present the threatening puzzle behind the glamour. But as the scene with George continues, she veers from behaviour which could seem acted out into a desperation that arises from a genuine annoyance at not being able to reach her husband. Since we do not yet know about her *Angst* over the astronauts, this sequence between the Moores re-creates a fairly normal thrust-and-parry between two people with a shared history and a fair knowledge of each other's habits and weaknesses but with insufficient regard for each other's inner bewilderment. This scene works because Stoppard has made Dotty George's intellectual match. As we soon discover, she had once been his student and she can laugh at her former career: "not at all bad for a one-time student amateur bored with keeping house for her professor" (39). Moreover, that intelligence and sense-of-self inform most of her remarks so that the characters pierce each other's guard and then, after a feint or two, resume the attack. Dotty's mind, and the energy it generates, makes her verbal thrusts seem entirely her own. Having dismissed George's claim to friendship with Bertrand Russell, she quickly stabs at his "living in a dreamland", and when he defensively turns that aside, she falls back dejectedly on the bed: "Oh God ... if only Archie would come" (31).

But it is their moments of stillness, rare in Stoppard, as the two reach across the gap between them, that move us nearest to who they are and persuade us that Dotty would not need Archie were George less unavailable. The stage directions indicate the characters' genuine feeling:

> DOTTY: I won't see him any more, if you like. (*Turns to him.*)
> I'll see you. If you like.
> (GEORGE *examines the new tone, and decides the moment is genuine.*)
> GEORGE (*softening*): Oh, Dotty ... The first day you walked into my class ... I thought, "*That's* better!" ... It was a wet day ... your hair was wet ... and I thought, "The hyacinth girl" ... and "How my hair is growing thin." (33)

Granted that the mood lasts only an instant, since George protects himself with bits from T. S. Eliot which Dotty picks up in gentle mockery, it does lead to their frankest interchange so far (Dotty is "in a bit of a spot") and to a relaxed affection. The climax of this scene, after more rounds of fencing, depends on a further instant of repose after Dotty bursts into hysteria and pictures George and herself under the moon of songwriters and poets. In tears, she clings to George who, bewildered and silent, can do nothing but stroke her hair, until it occurs to him that she may have seen Thumper. The question ruins the tenderness between them and, shamed though he is by his gaucherie, he has thrown one more chance away (41–2). However, in Act 2, an angry exchange proves just as convincing an indicator of the depth of feeling between them. That episode also adds to our sense of Dotty as her own person and qualifies our hitherto unreserved sympathies towards George who, from this point on, appears alarmingly naive and indecisive.

Oblivious to murder in his house and to repression on the streets, George emerges from the bathroom holding a dead goldfish whose bowl Dotty had commandeered for an earlier charade. Interestingly, the fish is called 'Archie', which suggests a shared joke at the latter's expense and fits well with the sort of detachment towards the whole psychiatric game that Dotty has displayed throughout the play. Shaking with rage, George calls Dotty a "murderous bitch", lamenting that the fish should have been murdered for the sake of a game:

> DOTTY (*angrily*): Murdered? Don't you dare splash *me* with your sentimental rhetoric! It's a bloody goldfish! Do you think every *sole meunière* comes to you untouched by suffering?
> GEORGE: The monk who won't walk in the garden for fear of treading on an ant does not have to be a vegetarian ...
> DOTTY: Brilliant! You must publish your findings in some suitable place like the *Good Food Guide*.
> GEORGE: No doubt your rebuttal would look well in the *Meccano Magazine*.
> DOTTY: You bloody humbug!—the last of the metaphysical

egocentrics! You're probably still shaking from the four-hundred-year-old news that the sun doesn't go round you! (74)

The way Dotty cuts through George's finer feelings and the way he delivers an equally smarting attack on what he takes to be her mechanistic views transform the play's philosophic debate into a lively marital quarrel, and Dotty's tirade leads naturally into her speech about the moon-landing's reduction of mankind, making it appear a spontaneous perception which wells up out of her anger (in *Another Moon* virtually the same speech had seemed imposed on Penelope). The irrationality behind their rage gives the clever dialogue a heartfelt drive. Had George listened to remarks like Dotty's "it's impossible to imagine anyone building a church on the moon" (39), he would know that her universe is not a mechanistic one; on the other hand, she is hardly the one to accuse George of being numbed by the planets. This sequence also ends in a climax of tears. Archie dismisses Dotty's emotion as mere emotion, "When did you first become aware of these feelings?" (75), yet Dotty calls out to "Georgie"—"*But* GEORGE *won't or can't ...*" Another chance of *rapprochement* has flown away on the winds.

At the end of the Act, George's remark about the monk who feared to step on an ant returns to plague him. Climbing down from his desk after discovering Thumper's fate, George accidentally steps back onto the carapace of Pat, the tortoise: "CRRRRRUNCH!!!" With one foot on the desk and one on Pat, he "puts up his head and cries out, 'Dotty! Help! Murder!'" (81). So the patterns of the play's main action are rounded off in the same way that they began, when George, faced with a corpse, cries out for help to a partner who makes no answer. Then, as George falls sobbing to the ground, *Jumpers* shifts into a dream sequence, just as it began with a seemingly surreal ritual.

—Anthony Jenkins, *The Theatre of Tom Stoppard*, (Cambridge: Cambridge University Press, 1987): pp. 92–95.

Paul Delaney on Moral Absolutes and God versus Moral Relativism

[Paul Delaney is Professor of English at Westmont College and the editor of *Tom Stoppard in Conversation* and *Brian Friel in Conversation*. Here he suggests that the play supports George's moral absolutism and conclusion that God exists over the Jumpers' moral relativism.]

After the intellectual dependence of the jumpers on McFee's moral relativism has been conclusively established, after George has laboured over riposte after riposte to McFee's premise, after an Inspector Bones has arrived on the scene investigating the murder of an acrobatic professor, after we have returned from intermission and are well into the second act, Stoppard finally chooses to disclose that the jumper shot out of the pyramid in the opening scene was—Duncan McFee. But not until the last moments of the second act do we learn that McFee had decided to defect from the ranks of the jumpers; that he had come to recognise the possibility of altruism, and—hence—the existence of good and evil; that he saw amorality as 'giving philosophical respectability to a new pragmatism in public life' which he found 'disturbing' (p. 70); and, in a crowning touch, that he was leaving the university, breaking off an affair with George's secretary, and entering a monastery!

I think we can now see why that image of the pyramid, which Stoppard terms the 'initial impetus for the play', proves so seminal. The moral relativism which McFee represents is the cornerstone for the positions of all the other jumpers. Their leaping to positions (philosophical or gymnastic) that can be held for the required length of time (about a minute for a gymnastic pyramid—maybe twenty minutes for a scholarly paper) is a form of academic gamesmanship founded on the moral relativism which McFee represents. There is a certain amount of fun in calling the philosophers jumpers and saying they will leap to any position. But the satire becomes keener when Stoppard reveals that any position the jumpers leap to will come crashing down as soon as one removes the premise that moral absolutes do not exist. If McFee defects, if the central premise that all value-judgements are relative is removed, the entire intellectual house of cards of the faddish philosophers comes tumbling down. It does not explode. Rather, it disintegrates because of lack of internal consistency; it collapses because of its own hollowness, the moral vacuousness which it has relied on instead of a core of values. The pyramid of gymnasts, Stoppard's stage directions tell us, 'has been defying gravity for these few seconds. Now it slowly collapses into the dark, imploding on the missing part, and rolling and separating, out of sight, leaving only the white spot' (p. 12).

If, then, we are to understand the play at all, we must first recognise that *Jumpers* affirms that moral absolutes do exist and, further, that the position of the jumpers who would deny such absolutes is—both literally and figuratively—undercut. (...)

Although Stoppard is attacking epistemological relativism, that last word serves as a stinging refutation of ethical relativism as well. More specifically Stoppard is attacking those 'Radical Liberal' political philosophers who have denied the spiritual nature of mankind and who would see humanity wholly in materialistic terms.

Stoppard then, is sure that Archie is wrong, that his 'materialistic argument'—Archie's own words (p. 60)—is invalid. Archie is the great high priest of the nihilistic jumpers, the archbishop of the Rad-Lib revolutionaries, the ever-guileful, ever-alluring archfiend. Of course Archie seems to be in control. The star of the Rad-Libs is in the ascendant. Even McFee at the point of his conversion acknowledges, 'I have seen the future, Henry, ... and it's yellow' (p. 71). That is, the future belongs to the extending influence of the yellow-clad jumpers who deny all moral absolutes. To see Archie as a spokesman for Stoppard's own beliefs is to misread the play utterly. (...)

After we acknowledge a level of certainty in the play—the certainty that the nihilistic, pragmatic materialism of Archie and the jumpers is invalid—it remains to be shown just what George, Stoppard's 'poor professor', got right and what he got wrong. There is a central debate, a sort of 'infinite leap-frog', in *Jumpers*; but the issue is not to be found between George on the one hand and the jumpers on the other. That is, what is at issue in the play should not be confused with what is at issue in the philosophy department's annual symposium on 'Man—good, bad or indifferent?' Rather, the point at stake shifts from the symposium's level of debate over whether moral absolutes exist, to the question of whether the moral absolutes—which do in fact exist—spring from a divine source or human experience: whether God is the progenitor of goodness or goodness is, a pre-existent absolute which precedes even God. This central tension of the work is also given intensely theatrical realisation. The entire stage is split between George in his study struggling to 'invent God' and Dotty in her bedroom on the verge of a nervous breakdown. (...)

But if George follows his convictions to ultimate conclusions he arrives, rather embarrassingly, at God. By midway in the second act, George's philosophical investigations have acquired new resonances, and the audience is properly hushed as he confesses his knowledge not just of the existence of moral absolutes but of a realm of the spirit which transcends both a Darwinian view of man as animal and a Marxist view of man as material:

> And yet I tell you that, now and again, not necessarily in the contemplation of rainbows or newborn babes, nor in extremities of pain or joy, but more probably ambushed by some quite trivial moment—say the exchange of signals between two long-distance lorry-drivers in the black sleet of a god-awful night on the old A1—then, in that dip-flash, dip-flash of headlights in the rain that seems to affirm some common ground that is not animal and not long-distance lorry-driving—then I tell you I *know*—I sound like a joke vicar, new paragraph. (p. 62)

Starting with the intuitive affirmation that human life is inherently moral, that human beings share 'some common ground that is not animal', George is impelled toward the irresistible conclusion that temporal moral values must imply the existence of a transcendent standard of moral perfection, that God—in a word—'is'. Taking a fresh start at conveying what he 'knows', George refers to the mathematical concept of 'a limiting curve, that is the curve defined as the limit of a polygon with an infinite number of sides' (p. 62). So, for example, if George takes an old threepenny-bit or a 50-pence piece and infinitely doubles the number of sides, he finds that a circle can be logically implied by the existence of polygons. With this new metaphor in mind George pushes beyond a perception of human spiritual communion to a sense of spiritual perfection:

> And now and again, not necessarily in the contemplation of polygons or newborn babes, nor in extremities of pain or joy, but more probably in some quite trivial moment, it seems to me that life itself is the mundane figure which argues perfection at its limiting curve. And if I doubt it, the ability to doubt, to question, to *think*, seems to be the curve itself. *Cogito ergo deus est.* (pp. 62–3)

Such an understanding of the limiting curve is, as John A. Bailey correctly points out, 'George's finest statement'. George's argument neither dismisses humanity as valueless nor offers a humanistic view that mankind is the measure of all values. Rather, George sees human imperfection. In effect he acknowledges that we live in a fallen world. But he still sees in that which is humanly possible a flawed figure which bodies forth the reflection of God. In the flashes of human communion with one's fellow man he senses an image of spiritual communion with God. And yet the evidence for this truth which he apprehends spiritually is so tenuous as to resist logical proof.

—Paul Delaney, *Tom Stoppard: The Moral Vision of the Major Plays*, (New York: St. Martin's Press, 1990): pp. 39–40, 41–42, 43, 45–46.

KATHERINE E. KELLY ON THE ROLE OF THE CODA

[Katherine E. Kelly is an Associate Professor of English at Texas A&M University. In addition to editing *Modern Drama by Women 1890s–1930s: An International Anthology*, she has also published articles on Samuel Beckett and T.S. Eliot. Here she describes the play's closing Coda as a lens through which the central themes are magnified. Ultimately, the Coda shows that art and the artist need the context of the world and can't simply exist for themselves.]

As George lies defeated on the floor of his study, holding his dead tortoise and hare, Stoppard borrows a convention from film, to suggest what follows. The prone George has a nightmare vision of the long-awaited Symposium on the question, "Man: Good, Bad or Indifferent?" Written in the form of a Coda, a formally distinct section of the play that summarizes with new emphasis elements of the first two acts, the dream sequence surrealistically distorts the characters and idioms we have already seen and heard. The disturbing quality of the distortion lies in its irrational mocking reduction, its burlesque, of the positions presented earlier, now rated by scorecards—9.7, 9.9, and so on.

Archie opens the Symposium speaking a nonsense academese that recapitulates George's theism:

Indeed, if moon mad herd instinct, is God dad the inference?—to take another point: If goons in mood, by Gad is sin different or banned good, fr'instance?—thirdly: out of the ether, random nucleic acid testes or neither unversa vice, to name but one—(73)

Written in a Joycean dialect (Whitaker compares the entire Coda to the Circe episode in *Ulysses* [1983, 98]), Archie's mockery translates something like: "If moon man has instinct, is the death of God to be inferred from it? To take another point: If good is in the moon [if God can be said to exist on the moon?], then is sin to be defined as a quality different from God or as the absence of good; thirdly, [has the universe arisen] either out of the ether or out of random mixing of gases, or neither [or] vice versa?" Archie follows George's earlier lead in separating the God of goodness from the God of creation, but says nothing coherent about either hypothesis. For logocentric George, such a mockery of philosophical argument is horrifying in prohibiting rebuttal.

Archie's sinister quality is more pronounced in the Coda,

which finally serves as a moral lens through which we review the central questions of the play. Since qualities like good and bad are, for Archie, anachronistic fictions, he openly dismisses all speculation on the subject of man's moral condition by observing merely that the human race is relatively happy. Archie expects nothing because he assumes nothing; he resists nothing but appears to comprehend everything. Thus his character, while theatrically entertaining in small doses, is finally one-dimensional.

The Coda also magnifies George's characteristic weakness. At a climactic moment, George stands by, refusing to interfere while Archbishop Clegthorpe is shot for failing to repudiate his belief in a supreme being. George's error replicates Guildenstern's: unwilling or unable to apply his humanism to human situations, to connect his belief in God to his judgment of how people should treat one another, George behaves like the "tame believer" of Archie's mockery—he becomes the powerless ivory-tower intellectual of Archie's description. As another of Stoppard's artist figures, George has failed to learn how to negotiate the boundary dividing art (here conceived as philosophical argument), from life (moon landings, distraught wives, power struggles). His attempts to solve his problem amount to ignoring the human ("real") world altogether. Thus he unwittingly proves Archie right: he is harmless.

Dotty appears to have done better than her male partners in the Coda, but the appearance is deceiving. In this dream state, she has regained her power of song, but her lyrics show her to be the same Dotty Moore who was broken by the demystifying of the moon. Dotty delivers her "philosophy" in her closing song: two and two make roughly four—generally speaking, we can assume that numbers will behave how we expect them to. However, judging by her own experience of men (both in and out of bed), they can be either good or bad but never neutral (— "Some ain't bad and some are revelations, / Never met indifference"). But how, asks Dorothy, can she be expected to believe in God? "Heaven, ... Just a lying rhyme for seven! / Scored for violins on multi-track" (77). God is a fictional disguise for chance made attractive by appeals to sentimentality. Firmly rooted in common sense and feeling, Dotty rejects metaphysical fictions as childish lies.

Finally, while Stoppard's sympathy belongs clearly to George and Dotty's struggle to refashion an intellectual and emotional center to contemporary life, he closes the play by suggesting that George, at least, has failed in that struggle not only because he could not find the words but also because he made his search for them its own justification. The implication of the Coda is glaringly apparent: art and the artist cannot exist for their own sakes alone. They are firmly embedded in the world around them and will always be used to some worldly end, perhaps a vicious end.

—Katherine E. Kelly, *Tom Stoppard and the Craft of Comedy: Medium and Genre at Play*, Theater: Text/Theory/Performance Series, (Ann Arbor, Mich.: University of Michigan Press, 1991): pp. 102–104.

PLOT SUMMARY OF

Travesties

Travesties' title offers a clue about its content, as there are indeed multiple travesties: of historical figures, of history, of memory, of *The Importance of Being Earnest*, and others. (The only exception is the Lenins, whose words are taken directly from their memoirs; they deliberately remain un-travestied). In reality, not all of the historical figures in the play—Henry Carr, James Joyce, Lenin, and Tristan Tzara—were in Zurich at the same time, although it is true that Carr starred as Algernon in Joyce's version of *Earnest* and that they sued each other. Historical accuracy aside, Stoppard's forum allows meetings between real-life people and fictional characters in order to examine views on art, patriotism and revolution. (Note that being familiar with Oscar Wilde's play, *The Importance of Being Earnest*, will be helpful in understanding plot points).

At the Zurich Public Library, Gwendolen Carr is attending to novelist James Joyce's dictation and Tristan Tzara the Dadaist is cutting up bits of paper with words on them, dropping them into a hat, and picking them at random to read aloud. This is punctuated every so often by Cecily the librarian's admonishing "Ssssssh!" Lenin is quietly writing. Cecily drops off some books for Lenin; he gives her a folder. Meanwhile, Joyce gives Gwendolen a folder. These folders are inadvertently switched. Nadya enters and tells her husband, in Russian, that St. Petersburg is having a revolution and the Tsar will abdicate.

The scene changes and Henry Carr, the play's narrator and now an old man, reminisces. We learn that Carr worked for the British Consulate. Then the scene flashes back to Carr as a young man talking to Bennett, his manservant. He asks Bennett what the papers say, and Bennett responds that they are mostly about the war. Carr bemoans Switzerland's neutrality, craving the visceral rawness of war.

This scene and much of the play is filtered through Old Carr's memory, which lapses every so often. These glitches make themselves known through repeating of lines. Carr again asks

Bennett about what's in the paper. This time, Bennett replies that there is a social revolution in Russia. When the question is asked next, Bennett says that the Tsar has abdicated.

Tzara, Gwendolen and Joyce arrive and all of them do their introductions as a limerick. Joyce, it's learned, has come to ask Carr for money to support a play he's putting on. The scene shifts and the characters mirror the patterns of their counterparts in *The Importance of Being Earnest*. (Carr confuses the events of the play with the events of his life).

Carr tells Tzara he was injured in the war and retreated to neutral Switzerland. They segue into a verbal repartee about art and its meaning; Tzara asserts that he is an artist, and is creating art, when cutting and rearranging other people's words. Tzara says that "art" can mean what you want it to mean; Carr doesn't agree. Carr further posits that wars are fought for artists to be safe, to which Tzara counters that wars are fought for monetary gain.

The scene restarts with Tzara's entrance (again). He tells Carr that he's been in the Public Library. Tzara is pleased to see that the table is set for tea with an extra cup for Gwendolen, Carr's sister. He tells Carr that he will propose to Gwendolen, whom he's been admiring from afar at the library.

Carr declares that he will not approve such a proposal from Tzara and the matter of "Jack" needs to be cleared up first. Tzara has left his library card at Carr's and the name on it is "Jack Tzara," not "Tristan Tzara," as Carr knows him (note that pseudonyms and mistaken identities is key to the plot of *Earnest*). Tzara explains that, when he was at a bar with Lenin, Lenin denounced the Dadaists as "decadent nihilists." So when Lenin introduced Tzara to Cecily at the library, she asked if he was the Dadaist Tzara. Tzara quickly replied that his younger brother Tristan was the Dadaist and signed up for his library card as "Jack Tzara."

Cecily, it turns out, is the "disciple" of Lenin in much the same way as Gwendolen is Tzara's disciple. The scene restarts and Gwendolen and Joyce enter. Joyce states he is there as a business manager, to say he is producing a British masterpiece play, *The Importance of Being Earnest*, and he asks Carr to play the leading role.

Carr assumes he will play Ernest; however, he is informed that he will play "the other one" (Algernon). Carr's first preoccupation is with the wardrobe of his character, so Joyce describes the play for him in terms of what he will be wearing for each scene. They leave to discuss the play.

Tzara confesses he has admired Gwendolen since he met her. She, in turn, confesses that she finds him fascinating because they both admire Joyce as an artist. When she found out he was a modern poet, she felt she was destined to love him. They embrace.

Joyce enters and interrogates Tzara on Dadaism and other Dadaists. Tzara wants "[t]he right to urinate in different colors" because "poetry should be as natural as making water." Joyce and Tzara get into an argument and Tzara says the time for Joyce's kind of literature has passed and that the new artists are vandals. Joyce tells Tzara that his urge for self-expression is beyond his artistic gifts and that *his* art—retelling Homer to bring double-the-immortality to the story of Ulysses—has life in it.

Henry, now reappearing as old Carr, remembers the lawsuit between he and Joyce. Carr sued Joyce for the cost of the suit he bought for the role and Joyce sued Carr for the cost of the play tickets Carr was supposed to sell. Joyce won the lawsuit, which Carr calls a "travesty of justice." A later lawsuit had Joyce suing Carr for slander, but that case was thrown out. Carr would've liked to cross-examine Joyce and ask what he did during the war: Joyce wrote *Ulysses* instead of fighting like Carr.

Act Two opens in the library with Cecily talking about Lenin. He wished to go to Russia, but the Allies saw him as a threat and didn't want him to leave Zurich.

Carr goes to the library and meets Cecily, who thinks that he is Tristan Tzara, the Dadaist. He is able to find out that she is helping to research Lenin's book on "Imperialism, the highest stage of capitalism." He also learns that Lenin will leave the country, in disguise and carrying false papers. Cecily confides to him that the Consul's manservant has radical tendencies. As Carr is the Consul, the manservant in question is Bennett, who has passed along Consulate correspondence to Tzara, also a radical.

Cecily concedes that she has wanted to reform Tristan Tzara "the decadent nihilist" since she heard about him from "Jack." They fall behind the library desk in embrace. Lenin and Nadya enter. Lenin dictates a letter to her telling of his plans to escape in disguise (wearing a wig) to Russia; Cecily and Carr are able to overhear his plans.

Tzara walks up to the library desk and rings the bell. Cicely jumps up and greets him as Jack. She tells him that his brother is there. Both men play along with the mistaken identities. Tzara introduces Carr to the Lenins as Tristan. Nadya talks of the new plan to get out of the country ... some Bolsheviks contacted the Germans and the Germans agreed to escort the Bolsheviks out of the country by special train.

Cecily waves goodbye to the Lenins' train as it leaves. Carr weighs whether or not to act on the information he has on the escaping Lenin. He decides to telegraph the Minister in Berne. The older Carr enters on the stage and states his predicament— much depended on whether he acted or didn't—Lenin got away. Carr feels he and Lenin agree on art (neither likes the "new art"), but it's the politics they can't agree on. Carr cannot agree with Tzara's and Joyce's view of art.

Gwendolen and Cecily meet and converse in song. Cecily is there to let Gwendolen know that Joyce has overdue library books on her card. In the course of their conversation, Cecily says that Tristan has given up art for the proletariat; Gwendolen claims that he is still doing art. The conversation becomes more heated until Carr appears. Cecily calls him Tristan, but Gwendolen tells Cecily that he is her brother, Henry Carr. Tzara enters and Gwendolen correctly calls him Tristan, while Cecily calls him Comrade Jack. Gwendolen and Cecily bond over the trick pulled on them by the men. They ask a question of the men: Cecily asks Carr his opinion of the essay she gave him ("as a social critique") to look at. Gwendolen asks Tzara what he thinks of the chapter ("as art for art's sake") she gave him to read. Both men agree that what they read was terrible.

Carr confronts Tzara by saying that he knows Bennett has been giving him Carr's own correspondence to read. Tzara doesn't deny it but says that Bennett has radical sympathies.

Bennett enters again, and in a scene that's been repeated, declares that the reviews for Carr's performance in *Earnest* were good.

Joyce arrives and demands money from Carr for the *Earnest* tickets; Carr counterclaims money for the suit. Tzara hands Joyce a folder. Joyce looks at it and all discover the mix-up of the folders. Everyone onstage embraces and starts to dance.

Carr and Cecily dance off-stage and Old Carr and Old Cecily dance back on. Old Cecily corrects Old Carr's recollection on a number of topics: there was a lawsuit involving trousers, but he never was close to Lenin. She doesn't remember "the other one" (Tzara). Lenin was already a leader when Carr played Algernon, but she didn't help Lenin write *Imperialism, the Highest Stage of Capitalism*, Carr was never Consul (actually, it was Bennett), and Sophia (not Gwendolen) married the artist. Carr becomes angry. He closes with, "I learned three things in Zurich during the war…. Firstly, you're either a revolutionary or you're not, and if you're not you might as well be an artist as anything else. Secondly, if you can't be an artist, you might as well be a revolutionary. I forget the third thing."

Travesties

(Note: *The Importance of Being Earnest* character equivalents are
in parentheses at the end of each description).

Henry Carr is an older gentleman through whose foggy
memory we see his younger self and the events of the play
unravel. He fights in World War I as a young man, but tellingly
describes some of his experiences in terms of the wardrobe he
was wearing at the time. Although he seems to appreciate fashion
(particularly in his "elegant" youth), his taste in the arts is
decidedly middle-class. After being wounded, he finds himself in
service to the British Consulate in Zurich. There James Joyce
approaches him about playing Algernon in his production of
Oscar Wilde's play *The Importance of Being Earnest*. Henry
performed his role ably; now, many years later, he confuses some
events in his life with the happenings in Wilde's play. He
remembers that he was sent to spy on Lenin and was too
indecisive to prevent Lenin from leaving Zurich, having been
distracted by his love for Cecily. Old Cecily corrects his
recollections at the end of the play. (Algernon)

Tristan Tzara is the young, short-and-boyish-looking Dadaist
poet who wears a monocle. He literally cuts up existing poetry
(like that of Shakespeare) and randomly draws the paper cuttings
from a hat to make new poems. Carr disagrees with Tzara's
disregard for the concreteness of language and what it stands for.
Tzara is enamored by Henry's sister Gwendolen and wishes to
propose to her. At the library, he passes himself off as his fictious
older brother Jack Tzara so that his identity as a Dadaist is not
revealed. He has Bolshevik leanings and carries inside
information to Lenin. (Jack)

James Joyce, the thirty-six-year-old author of *Ulysses*, is a more
traditional artist. Through his novel, he seeks to celebrate and
"redouble the renown" of Homer's *Odyssey*. He disagrees with
Tzara's destructive approach to art. He cuts a rather interesting

figure, though, wearing mismatched jacket and trousers from two sets of suits. (Lady Augusta Bracknell)

Gwendolen Carr is Henry Carr's younger sister and a devotee of James Joyce who is pursued by Tristan Tzara. She is young, attractive, and a "personality to be reckoned with." (Gwendolen)

Cecily Carruthers is a librarian with Bolshevik leanings and a unique repertoire of learning, as she has read books alphabetically starting with "A." Fond of shushing the library's patrons, she falls for Henry Carr when he comes into the library masquerading as "Tristan Tzara" the Dadaist. She has notions of "saving" the artist, so they begin a romance and she eventually marries Henry Carr. In the last scene, Cecily—referred to as "Old Cecily," as she is indeed much older—corrects her husband's erroneous memories of his life. (Cecily)

Bennett is remembered as Carr's manservant with radical tendencies who passed on Carr's correspondence to Tzara; Old Cecily tells us he was actually the Consul. (Lane)

Vladimir Ilyich Lenin or "Lenin" is the late-forties Bolshevik leader and a man of action. He speaks formally and comes across as cold. The only time the emotionless mask is cracked is when his wife describes him or when he explains his tearful and heartfelt response to hearing the *Appassionata*. He spends a lot of time in Zurich's Public Library, until he is told by his wife that there is a revolution in St. Petersburg. The couple escape in a sealed train to Russia.

Nadezhda Krupskaya or "Nadya" is Lenin's wife. She, like her husband, does not have her words or actions travestied, as they come directly from her (or Lenin's) memoirs. It is through her that we see a more emotional side of Lenin.

CRITICAL VIEWS ON
Travesties

RICHARD CORBALLIS ON THE ROLE OF MEMORY

[In this excerpt, Corballis examines how Carr's unreliable memory affects the structure of the play, its artifice, and its blending of source texts and styles.]

The potential significance of *The Importance of Being Earnest* is indicated by the fact that Carr gets on to the subject of his 'personal triumph in the demanding role of Ernest, not Ernest, the other one' almost at once. His more general susceptibility to artistic licence is indicated obviously enough in a number of ways. Firstly, he makes a quite explicit attempt to present his memories as formal memoirs, and when he runs off the rails he is happy to assert blithely, 'that's the art of it'. Secondly, to introduce these memoirs he adopts a highly artificial style—or rather series of styles, oxymoron dominating the portrait of Joyce, poetic language that of Lenin and travel-brochure-ese (as in Arthur's monologue in *New-Found-Land*) that of Tzara and the Dada-ists. In each case the artifice is interrupted by Carr's own eccentric and bigoted voice. On the one hand this serves to stress the degree of distortion going on. On the other hand, however, it reminds us that Old Carr, as opposed to Young Carr and the other 'clockwork' figments of his doting mind, is a *real* character like the Lenins. We shall need to ponder his reality—and Old Cecily's—when we come to consider the dialogue between these two which ends the play. For the moment, however, it is the artifice of the dreams rather than the reality of the dreamer that is emphasized. This artifice is accentuated by his habit of relying on artificial aids to memory, particularly photographs. Joyce is visualized 'in a velvet smoking jacket of an unknown colour, photography being in those days a black and white affair'. This of course proves that Carr saw the smoking jacket only in photographs and therefore cannot have known the man very well. He is talking here about the post-Zürich Joyce so there is some justification for his ignorance. Carr is rather more open about his reliance on photographs to visualize Lenin, and we should realize long before the end of the play that Carr never saw Lenin in the flesh. Photography is not necessary as an aid in Tzara's case since Carr hardly seems capable of distinguishing between Tzara and a host of other artists from 'tween the before-the-war-to-end-all-wars years and the between-the-wars years'. This part of the monologue is spent fooling around with a series of literary and sub-literary puns, which again indicate the extent to which art is triumphing over reality. Finally, we get an apostrophe to 'Switzerland, the still centre of the wheel of war', which contrives to make the very setting of the play seem utterly divorced from reality. (Stoppard adopted a similar attitude to Switzerland when he came to write the first scene of *The Real Thing* some ten years later.)

When at last the dialogue gets under way the artificial control imposed by Old Carr's memory continues to be evident. The scene with Bennett is modelled on Algernon's scene with Lane at the beginning of *The Importance of Being Earnest*, and there is a good deal of borrowing from other authors too—in Carr's big speech just before the second time-slip, for example. But the artifice is not confined to the surface of the text. Old Carr is not just embroidering past events; he is significantly distorting them, as Nabokov's senile or deranged narrators are wont to do (e.g. in *Despair*) and as Peter Shaffer's Salieri *fails* to do in *Amadeus* (which is one reason why that play is less satisfying than *Travesties*). At the end of the play Old Cecily cajoles Old Carr into revealing that the alleged master–servant relationship between himself and Bennett is a false one, since Bennett was in fact the British Consul in Zürich and Carr his underling. Here, then, is another artificial barrier between the audience and the true events of 1918. Yet another is provided by the celebrated time-slips when 'Old Carr's memory, which is not notably reliable ... drops a scene' so that 'the story (like a toy train perhaps) ... jumps the rails and has to be restarted at the point where it goes wild'. And if this device is accentuated, as Stoppard suggests it might be, by 'the sound of a cuckoo-clock, artificially amplified', then we are given, as in a number of Stoppard's other works, a literal demonstration of the 'clockwork' of these episodes.

Artifice continues to dominate as we witness the arrivals of Tzara, Joyce and Gwendolen, which are patterned on the entrances of Jack, Lady Bracknell and Gwendolen in the first act of *The Importance of Being Earnest*. Actually the arrival of these three characters is presented twice by Stoppard, first in a compressed and hilariously artificial form with Tzara/Jack depicted as 'a Rumanian nonsense' and Joyce initiating a whole scene couched in limericks, and then at greater length with all the characters speaking urbane, Wildean English. Of course, the very duplication of these entrances proves how artificial everything is at this point. (...)

So far, then, with one brief exception, the worlds of art and politics have been kept quite separate and it might seem that Tynan is right to insist that 'The hard polemic purpose of *Travesties* is to argue that art must be independent of politics'. But what looks on paper like a delicate balance between the two forces is disturbed on the stage by the fact that the Lenins enjoy a closer liaison with the audience than do the artists, who are bloodless figments of Old Carr's imagination. This imbalance becomes even more marked in the closing moments of the play. The travesty of *The Importance of Being Earnest* concludes with a dance for all concerned, which effects 'a complete dislocation of the play'. What follows is, given the precedent of *Jumpers*, probably best described as a coda. Old Carr reappears on stage, accompanied by a new character—Old Cecily. Their dialogue has the initial effect of spelling out still more emphatically the dislocation between art and politics. Old Cecily quickly establishes that Carr never saw Lenin and that he was never the Consul.[1] These discoveries serve to confirm what we should have grasped already: that the Lenin sequences in *Travesties* are historically authentic whereas the Joyce/Tzara/Gwendolen/Carr sequences are the artificial product of Old Carr's erratic memory. But there is more to this passage than a simple reinforcement of the art/politics dichotomy. Old Cecily's determined attack upon her husband's memory inevitably has the effect of devaluing the airy visions which that memory has conjured up. True, Old Cecily provides, for the *literati*, muted support for the endeavours of art early in the coda when she describes her betrothal to Carr in words which recall Molly Bloom's famous affirmative at the end of *Ulysses*: '... and yes, I said yes when you asked me ...' But thereafter all her energies are devoted to sorting out the facts, and eventually her determined realism rubs off on Carr whose final speech ends not with the artificial bang, which we might have expected, but with a realistic whimper. His words echo those of Nadya's last speech, delivered earlier, as well as the last words of *Dogg's Our Pet* and the first words of Beckett's *The Unnameable*:

> I learned three things in Zürich during the war. I wrote them down. Firstly, you're either a revolutionary or you're not, and if you're not you might as well be an artist as anything else. Secondly, if you can't be an artist, you might as well be a revolutionary ... I forget the third thing.

The build-up to that last sentence is much funnier than the build-up to Nadya's 'I forget what', but the parallel still serves to invest Old Carr with a tattered dignity, which is akin to that of George Riley and George Moore.

It is really only now that we can fully appreciate the engaging reality of Old Carr and distinguish it from the slick 'clockwork' of his dreams. But if we look back over the play from this vantage-point we can see that poor, lovable, bumbling Old Carr was always in evidence behind the airy fantasies of Act I. Consider the time-slips, for example. As we have seen, they provide proof positive that what we are watching in Act I is an artificial construct emanating from Old Carr's mind. But when we ask ourselves what causes these time-slips we generally find that it is the pressure of some particularly vivid memory which Old Carr wishes to suppress. (Shades of 'Prufrock' again; indeed 'Prufrock' is quoted just before the first time-slip.) So paradoxically, while the device signals a high level of artifice or 'clockwork', it also indicates that reality, in the form of the dreamer's subconscious, is endeavouring to break through this facade. In fact, in their small way the time-slips give the lie to the common complaint that there is no real dramatic conflict in *Travesties*.

NOTE

1. She rather spoils her no-nonsense image by maintaining that Tzara's girlfriend was called Sophia and not Gwendolen; in fact her name was Maya Chrusecz. Stoppard would seem to be guilty of jeopardizing coherence for the sake of a pun on women's names and European capital cities. Another important problem with Cecily is that she exists outside Old Carr's memory as both Young Cecily (at the beginning of Act II) and Old Cecily (at the end).

—Richard Corballis, *Stoppard, the Mystery and the Clockwork*, (New York: Methuen, 1984): pp. 80–82, 92–94.

TIM BRASSELL ON THE SYMBOLISM OF THE CHARACTERS

[Tim Brassell was Literature and Publicity Officer with Northern Arts in Newcastle upon Tyne and editor of *Arts North* newspaper. Here, he explores the characters' roles as they relate to the theme of art and revolution. He concludes that Stoppard comes down on the side of artists who are free of dogmatism.]

Stoppard is primarily concerned with the concepts of art and revolution and the possible relationship between them. Inside the frame established by Carr runs a broad-based discussion of these two subjects in which each character has a clear-cut contribution to make. Lenin is presented as a man of absolute commitment to action, burning with fervent determination to implement the theories he has spent his life formulating. Joyce demonstrates a scarcely lesser commitment to his art, and pursues it with a passion and conviction that verge upon religious dedication. Tzara exemplifies the artist's zealous commitment to the destruction of the false and outmoded gods of established culture. In addition, Lenin holds important views on art, Tzara on revolution. Between them the three provide a wealth of possibilities and opportunities, but without any self-evident focal point. It is Young Carr's role as prompter and catalyst which provides this, as his trenchant and reactionary views fuel—not to say inflame—the various stages of the debate. Unlike *Jumpers*, the rôle of the central character therefore exists both outside the action—as Old Carr, presenting his fabricated portrait of Zurich—and within it, as Young Carr, an active combatant in a similar sense to George in his pitched battle against the legions of Logical Positivism. (...)

For much of the second half of the play, the solemn, towering figure of Lenin unquestionably restricts the comic momentum, weakening in particular the overall effect of the *Earnest* pastiche. Yet we can now see this as a risk which Stoppard deliberately takes, for one of his major concerns is precisely to suggest how art can be overshadowed and even controlled by the currents of political activity—even when his own brilliance may be jeopardised in the process. In this way the rôle of Lenin completes the intermittent debate on art and revolution; even though he never converses with the other characters, his is the most important single contribution. Like Carr, he regards the notion of the artist-magician heralded by Joyce as anathema, but for quite different reasons:

> Down with literary supermen! Literature must become a part of the common cause of the proletariat ...

> The freedom of the bourgeois writer, artist or actor is simply disguised dependence on the money-bag, on corruption, on prostitution. Socialist literature and art will be free because the idea of socialism and sympathy with the working people will bring ever new forces to its ranks. (p. 85)

Here, and throughout the act, Stoppard's approach is to use Lenin's own recorded statements whenever possible so that he may stand condemned, literally, by his own words. Behind his insistence that the artist's true freedom can emerge only through decisive political change is, of course, his obsessive and singular concern with that political change. Unlike the other main characters of *Travesties*, he has no first-hand knowledge of the processes that make individuals produce art and its ambiguous importance to him personally is further shown in Stoppard's final quotation, which Lenin delivers to the background swell of Beethoven's *Appassionata*:

> I don't know of anything greater than the Appassionata. Amazing, superhuman music. It always makes me feel, perhaps naively, it makes me feel proud of the miracles that human beings can perform. But I can't listen to music often. It affects my nerves, makes me want to say nice stupid things and pat the heads of those people who while living in this vile hell can create such beauty. Nowadays we can't pat heads or we'll get our hands bitten off. We've got to hit heads, hit them without mercy, though ideally we're against doing violence to people ... Hm, one's duty is infernally hard. (p. 89)

This is the decisive verdict Stoppard has sought from his character. There must be no miracles and no beauty; in the final analysis, art is seen as a potential counter-revolutionary force, uniting or at least emasculating those who should consider themselves enemies. As such, whether it is the art of Joyce or of Tzara, it must be resisted until something new can take its place.

Stoppard has suggested that 'ideological differences are often temperamental differences in ideological disguise' and the stifling dominance of 'Socialist Realism' in post-revolutionary Russia can certainly be traced to Lenin's own views on art. One man's idiosyncratic beliefs can thus be transformed into an orthodoxy laying claim to an absolute moral righteousness and *Travesties* uses Lenin to show how political dictatorship—in whatever guise—must include artistic dictatorship. No doctrine in fact cuts deeper into the notions of artistic freedom and, as Carr declares early in the play,

> The easiest way of knowing whether good has triumphed over evil is to examine the freedom of the artist. (p. 39)

This, surely, amounts to Stoppard's own view and his concern, underlying the whole of *Travesties*, is whether artists of any persuasion can survive in a climate dominated by a man such as Lenin. In a special sense, therefore, the play does not merely circumnavigate the beliefs of the three main characters: it arranges them in such a fashion as to spotlight the various directions open to twentieth-century art. Joyce, though his own art is done scant justice, provides the yardstick by which the more traditional art is continually re-shaped; Tzara, though his own 'art' is contradictory and destructive, provides the yardstick by which it is subjected to constant challenge; Lenin, as an absolute dogmatist, provides a yardstick by which art is throttled in the grip of political intolerance, and it is towards his direct challenge to the artist that Stoppard relentlessly draws our attention in the second half of the play. Lenin is, of course, free to love the *Appassionata* and hate Dadaism, just as Tzara is free to do the opposite, but Tzara did not force his views onto a nation of several hundred million people. Stoppard's' concern is over the vulnerability of the artist's freedom.

> Aren't you ashamed for printing 5000 copies of Mayakovsky's new book? It is nonsense, stupidity, double-dyed stupidity and affectation. I believe such things should be published one in ten, and not more than 1500 copies, for libraries and cranks. As for Lunacharsky, he should be flogged for his futurism. (p. 87)

These words—Lenin's own in a memo to the Commissar for Education in 1919—point towards repression, not change, and the sixty succeeding years have demonstrated their importance. (...)

Lenin's political aim is definite, defined, but he summons art to follow, as it cannot. Joyce and Tzara are not revolutionaries in this sense, and cannot be. Stoppard lauds the rights of the artist and opposes the cruelty and immorality of imposing dogmatism upon them, and though the character of Lenin who personifies this dogmatism is without precedent in any of his previous plays, his shadow is firmly cast over several of those that follow.

—Tim Brassell, *Tom Stoppard: An Assessment*, (New York: St. Martin's Press, 1985): pp. 140–141, 158–161, 162.

[In this excerpt, Jenkins criticizes the use of Carr as an unreliable narrator as well as the over-use of jokes, puns and limericks to draw attention to the style of the play, trivializing its content.]

The failure of *Travesties*, therefore, is not the result of its zany mix of styles, since the library scene immediately establishes and supports that stylistic hodgepodge, nor can it be blamed on the counterpoint between travestied characters like Joyce and Tzara and those like the Lenins who basically appear as their historical selves, although the latter pair do tend to travel (literally and metaphorically) in an enclosed compartment. As his final words indicate, the alliance between the play's farcical action and serious ideas ends in divorce because of Old Carr. Where the play depicts the artist as a type of revolutionary, Carr amusingly sees them as opposites and—more damagingly—shrugs off their whole debate with the 'so what?' attitude that also colours his version of every serious argument between the characters whom he derails in explosions of personal invective.

Had the action been stage-managed by a more translucent narrator, *Travesties* might stand ironically as Stoppard's most Brechtian fable, with its snatches of song and dance, open stage, self-contained episodes, dialectical argument, and undisguised theatricality. But given the subjective quirkiness of Carr, each character's independent point of view is subverted by a narrator whose own attitude is epitomized by his attraction to *The Importance of Being Earnest* as an opportunity for several changes of costume and for whom the Great War (between nations or between himself and Joyce) centres upon the quality of one's trousers. Yet the ideas in *Travesties* cannot be shrugged aside as so much dandified nonsense. It surely does matter that though the artistic revolutionary, unlike his political counterpart, has no immediate effect on society, it is his work which ultimately shapes our ethics because he refuses to submit to the State. For though the artist may appear "irresponsible" when he demands, as Tzara does, "the right to urinate in different colours" (61), given Lenin and the Marxists' sense of social responsibility "multi-coloured micturition is no trick to those boys, they'll have you pissing blood" (83).

It is Carr who says that, but the terror of this remark in no way effects his older self, and so the idea is reduced to a snappy one-liner. This is characteristic of much of *Travesties*. Jokes and puns fly out at us in rapid profusion. Lines like "jewelled escapements and refugees of all kinds" (23) or the description of "a Swiss redlight district, pornographic fretwork shops, vice dens, get a grip on yourself" (24) make inventive and, at each given moment, effective detours into Carr's jackdaw mind. But at other times, the jokes are either so elaborate as to lose their point in the theatre, as when Tzara's pieced-together nonsense poem turns out, if one takes the time to wrestle with it, to make considerable sense in French (for example, "noon avuncular ill day Clara" (18) converts into "'nous n'avons que l'art', il déclara") or they simply go on too long. The limerick sequence in Act I or Gwendoline and Cecily's later "Mr Gallagher and Mr Shean" routine stretch out to the point of self-indulgence, while the prolonged interview between Tzara and Joyce (a parody of the catechism in *Ulysses* and Lady Bracknell's interrogation of Mr Worthing) halts the action in order to deliver undiluted information about Dadaism, a tactic as diversionary as Cecily's much-criticized sermonette on Lenin. In all these cases, the play's style draws our attention away from its content or back to the self-regarding Carr, who like some rusted Lord Malquist, withdraws from chaos with style. But, however entertaining that might be, the old man's egocentric and barren version of history eventually trivializes the central idea that the artist's independent vision and humanity turns fact into spiritual gold.

—Anthony Jenkins, *The Theatre of Tom Stoppard*, (Cambridge: Cambridge University Press, 1987): pp. 123–124.

PAUL DELANEY ON LANGUAGE

[In this excerpt, Delaney explores the characters' relationship with language to illuminate the art/revolution theme of the play. He concludes that

Lenin's and Tzara's abuse and twisting of language points to their immorality.]

Whereas Lenin's position self-destructs and Tzara proves a mere cut-up, Stoppard has made clear on numerous occasions that he infinitely prefers, he 'absolutely', 'categorically' agrees with Joyce. 'Lenin', Stoppard says, 'keeps convicting himself out of his own mouth. It's absurd.... It's sheer nonsense! However, the playwright adds elsewhere, 'Lenin had no use for the kind of art represented by Dada, which is one of the few things Lenin and I agree on': 'Writing a poem by taking words out of a hat may be amusing fun, but let's not call the result poetry.' 'What it isn't', Stoppard continues, 'is art'. 'I have no interest in anarchic or unstructured art', Stoppard declares, 'I have no sympathy at all with Tristan Tzara'. By contrast, 'Joyce is an artist I can respect' and admire as 'the finest practitioner of a style of literature with which I temperamentally agree'. 'It just happens that I'm on his side', Stoppard asserts, prompting his interlocutor's question as to what side that may be: 'The side of logic and rationality. And craftsmanship.'

Coppélia Kahn argues that whatever side Stoppard may be on, *Travesties* itself does not take sides: 'Though Stoppard insistently poses the question of the social role of art, he refuses to answer it. He mocks Joyce's Homeric high priest of art and Tzara's barbaric yawper and Lenin's "cog in the Social Democratic mechanism" with equal gusto and wit.' Similarly, Allan Rodway claims that 'no principle of decision is made available' in *Travesties* for valuing Joyce more than Lenin. However, Stoppard does not merely say that he personally agrees with one side of a debate which is presented with disinterested objectivity within the play. 'I happen to be on his side', Stoppard reiterates, 'which is why I've given Joyce the last word'. 'Consciously or not', Stoppard continues, 'I loaded the play for him'. As we should see, an affirmation of Joycean craftsmanship rather than Dadaist anti-art or Marxist-Leninist functional art is not merely dependent on authorial pronouncements outside the play but on internal evidence which permeates *Travesties*. (...)

Just as Tzara's contradictory and unreal notions about the

world begin in his own self-absorption in his identity as an artist, the confusions which Lenin and Lenin's ideological disciple Cecily express about the nature of art and society arise from their failure to apprehend reality in its complex wholeness. Cecily's knowledge is literally (and here again Stoppard has literalised metaphor) encyclopaedic: 'her knowledge of the poets, *as indeed of everything else*, is eccentric, being based on alphabetical precedence' (p. 42, emphasis mine). It begins in the encyclopaedia, with strict definitions. Whereas Tzara defies any definition, and uses words for whatever purposes he pleases, Cecily mistakes words for absolute, concrete realities.

In this she follows Lenin, who, like Cecily, based his knowledge of life, his approach to life, on a bookish intellectualism invalidated by experience. A university student reading Marx as devoutly as he had prepared for his high school final examinations (p. 68), Lenin uncritically accepted Marx's false premise that 'people were a sensational kind of material object' (pp. 76–7) and Marx's false assumption that the classes would inexorably move further apart, a result demonstrable in every way but experience by the 'inexorable working-out of Marx's theory of capital' (p. 76). Lenin's revolutionism is not based on the needs of the masses, but on his own abstract systematic theory divorced from life. Cecily tells Henry that Lenin refused to help organise famine relief because 'he understood that the famine was a force for the revolution' (p. 77). That is, because of an intellectual system conceived privately, he refused to respond to real need. His theoretical perception drove out the reality of the suffering of those whom he intended to save.

Just so, Lenin's ideological dictum, reiterated by Cecily, that 'the sole duty and justification for art is social criticism' (p. 74) drives out the reality of his own visceral response to art. Tzara informs Henry that Lenin flew into a rage against the Dadaists when someone began to play a sonata by Beethoven, the very archetype of romantic individualism. Although his ideology would deny the value or even ability of art to elevate or transport the human soul, which his theory would also deny, upon hearing the 'Appassionata' Lenin can be transported to consideration of the 'superhuman', 'the miracles that human beings can perform', the creation of 'beauty' (p. 89).

Lenin's ideology must postulate a collective ethic divorced from its effect on individual lives. Correspondingly, he promulgates a freedom apart from anything that can be experienced by an individual. Thus he affirms a 'free press' but one which will be *free from bourgeois anarchist individualism!* (p. 85). In effect, Lenin, with all the totalitarian zeal if not the humour of President Mageeba in *Night and Day*, affirms a 'relatively free press', a press which will have about as much freedom as one edited by Mageeba's relatives. Hence Lenin involves himself in impossible convolutions of logic, mistaking the terms of his intellectual system for concrete realities. The world of experience is subjected to textbook definitions. Words become arbitrary, dictatorial—just as they do in Tzara's verbal anarchy.

By their words we know them. And in *Travesties* both Lenin and Tzara are convicted by their language. If one of the serious themes in *Jumpers*, as Ronald Hayman correctly notes, is the 'connection between immorality and imprecision in the use of language', *Travesties* leads us to see Lenin and Tzara not only as imprecise in their twisting of words but immoral. Their unscrupulous abuse of language reflects their pervasive lack of scruple. *Travesties*, then, unequivocally answers the question it raises as to whether an artist and a revolutionary can be one and the same person. Lenin may be a revolutionary; but his own visceral response to art demonstrates that his aesthetic theories self-destruct. Tzara, who aspires to be both revolutionary artist and artistic revolutionary, evinces instead political paralysis and artistic aridity. *Travesties* demonstrates conclusively that the revolutionary cannot hope to change the world by pulling random words out of a hat nor can the artist hope to dance within the strait-jacket of ideology. (...)

It is Carr who defends the objective meaning of language against Tzara's attempts to twist words to mean whatever he wishes them to mean. 'If there is any point in using language at all', Carr insists, 'it is that a word is taken to stand for a particular fact or idea and not for other facts or ideas' (p. 38). In this, Carr is also a forerunner of another Henry who in *The Real Thing* will demolish another 'radical' attempt to redefine language. 'Words don't deserve that kind of malarkey', asserts Henry (not Carr, the other one), 'they're innocent, neutral, precise, standing for this, describing that, meaning the other' (p. 54). (...)

Carr and Joyce are natural allies. Carr objects to the abuse of language and Joyce is the conserver and renewer of language. Joyce is embarked, in *Ulysses*, on a monumental exaltation of the common life of humanity and Carr is a common human. Carr has sympathy with the underdog and Joyce, an impoverished writer afflicted with numerous eye ailments, private penury and public rejection, is downtrodden. Both also know that civilisation and the arts are connected. 'Wars are fought to make the world safe for artists. It is never quite put in those terms but it is a useful way of grasping what civilised ideals are all about' (p. 39), Carr tells Tzara. 'The temples are built and brought down around him, continuously and contiguously, from Troy to the fields of Flanders. If there is any meaning in any of it, it is in what survives as art.... What now of the Trojan War if it had been passed over by the artist's touch? Dust ...' declaims Joyce (p. 62). The views supplement each other. Wars are fought for freedom of artistic expression; the artist transfigures and preserves society imaginatively because it cannot be preserved physically. But a pervasive irony of the work is that although Carr and Joyce are natural allies, they never recognise each other as such. Joyce requires the material assistance and the political freedom which Carr can help provide; Carr needs the qualities of imagination and intellect with which Joyce is gifted. (...)

Can the artist and the revolutionary be one and the same person? Quite clearly the final words of *Travesties* answer in the negative. One is either an artist or one is a revolutionary. One is either a revolutionary or one is an artist. But a 'revolutionary artist'? That is a thing of nought. The very concept is not worth remembering. The first two points deny its very existence. 'I forget the third thing'. What is there to be besides being a revolutionary or being an artist? The third thing is to be Henry Carr, to be an ordinary human being; because even revolutionaries and artists are only Henry Carrs, only Leopold Blooms. When they attempt to assert the contrary, to destroy the Carr-ness in humanity, they become inhuman, self-contradictory, dangerous. Lenin *'wasn't Lenin then'*; nor is he ever the Lenin of history. Neither is Joyce the figure James Joyce, nor Tzara the Dadaist Tristan Tzara. That each person is like Bloom the hero of his own life, and yet each is an extraneous ordinary person, in spite of his achievements, is the third thing; and it binds the play together and caps the intricate vigorous unity of *Travesties*.

—Paul Delaney, *Tom Stoppard: The Moral Vision of the Major Plays*, (New York: St. Martin's Press, 1990): pp. 62–63, 65–67, 70, 77, 79, 81.

PLOT SUMMARY OF

Arcadia

Some critics laud *Arcadia* as Stoppard's finest play, in which an intellectual storyline is populated with believable, developed characters with heart. These characters are able to comment on the intersection and finer points of scientific principles, the history of garden design, and the chaotic nature of sexual attraction.

The play opens on a stately English house situated at the edge of a garden in the year 1809. Sitting at a table, tutor Septimus Hodge and his pre-teen pupil, Thomasina Coverly, attend to their studies. She suddenly asks him what "carnal embrace" means and he responds that it is "the practice of throwing one's arms around a side of beef." Her inquiry stemmed from overhearing that Mrs. Chater, wife of the poet Ezra Chater, was caught in "carnal embrace" with someone (not her husband) in the gazebo. Septimus explains briefly what "carnal embrace" means, but leaves out that *he* was the one caught with Mrs. Chater.

The question sparks a conversation between teacher and pupil about sex and love, free will and self-determination, science and belief. Thomasina observes that jam, when stirred in rice pudding, can only be stirred so the jam becomes increasingly pink. Afterward, the jam can't be "unstirred" from the pudding; it is a one-way process only.

Their discussion is interrupted by Mr. Chater, who is upset over Septimus' affair with his wife and challenges him, but Septimus expertly flatters Mr. Chater as a "first rank poet" and defuses the situation around quickly. In the end, Chater thinks his wife slept with the tutor to gain a good review for his book, *The Couch of Eros*. Chater takes up a pen and signs the front of Septimus' copy of the book, 'To my friend Septimus Hodge....'

Noakes the landscape designer arrives. Right behind him is Lady Croom and Captain Brice, who opens Mr. Noakes' sketchbook. In it, there are watercolors of the surrounding garden with "before" and "after" representations. Thomasina pronounces the picturesque style "perfect" and reminiscent of Salvator Rosa, the painter. Lady Croom is upset that the plans include turning the refined and orderly English garden into a wild and irregular arrangement of forest, crags and briars. Even the gazebo would be replaced by a hermitage. Lady Croom declares that the current state of Sidley Park is "nature as God intended" and she can say 'Et in Arcadia ego!' or 'Here I am in Arcadia.'

All assembled are interupted from their discussion by the distant sound of guns and a pigeon shoot. Septimus revisits Lady Croom's translation as 'Even in Arcadia, there am I.' (This is a reference to Poussin's famous painting of idyllic shepherds who discovers a tombstone with the Latin engraving, that could suggest that Death is in Arcadia). Thomasina walks over to the sketchbook, pen in hand, and draws a hermit at the hermitage. She delivers a note to Septimus from Mrs. Chater, which he reads, folds and puts between the pages of *The Couch of Eros*.

The second scene takes place in the same room in the Sidley Park mansion, but in the present time. Researcher Hannah Jarvis is paging through Noakes' sketchbook. Chloë, the daughter of the house, bursts into the room with Bernard Nightingale, a critic looking for information on Ezra Chater. He asks to have his name withheld from Hannah and Chloë complies. Bernard thinks Hannah is writing a book on the garden; Valentine says she's writing about hermits. Hannah enters, calling Bernard "Peacock," the pseudonym Chloë has given him.

Bernard flatters Hannah about her book on Lady Caroline Lamb, Lord Byron's mistress, but she isn't interested until Bernard mentions the name of Ezra Chater and his connection to Sidley Park. To illustrate his point, Bernard shows her the copy of *The Couch of Eros* with its inscription Chater wrote to Septimus Hodge. Bernard asks Hannah for leads on either man to inform a speech he will be giving. They discuss the members of the household and Bernard learns Valentine is a mathematician, Gus is the quiet one, and their mother is studying and excavating the garden.

Hannah mentions the Sidley hermit that she's researching as a "peg for the nervous breakdown of the Romantic Imagination" and proceeds to show Bernard the hermit's likeness in Noakes' sketchbook. She explains that when the hermit died, the hermitage was found to be stuffed with stacks of papers covered with "cabalistic proofs." The hermit, she says, symbolizes the decline from the thinking of the Enlightenment to the feeling of the Romantic.

Bernard, still interested in Byron and Chater, asks to look through Hannah's source materials. Chloë breezes through the room and absentmindedly refers to Bernard as "Mr. Nightingale," whereupon Hannah recognizes him as the author who wrote a terrible review of her book. Hannah is angry, but Bernard wins her over. The copy of *The Couch of Eros* originally belonged to Septimus Hodge, but was found in Lord Byron's library and Bernard notes that the underlined passages correspond exactly to excerpts from a review in the *Piccadilly Recreation* panning *The Couch of Eros*. Bernard reads Hannah three notes that were found in the book, all pertaining to guns and hinting of a duel, so he concludes that Byron killed Chater. They discover Septimus and Byron were classmates at Trinity College. Bernard, overjoyed, kisses Hannah on the cheek.

Chloë witnesses the kiss, and suspecting that it was caused by sparks of romance, offers to ask Bernard to the impending dance for Hannah. Hannah isn't interested in Bernard as a dance partner, to which Chloë replies that her "genius brother" (Gus) will be relieved, as he is in love with Hannah. Gus appears with an apple just picked from the garden and hands it to Hannah.

In Scene Three's 1809 setting, Thomasina is ploddingly translating a passage from Latin, when she suddenly tells Septimus that her mother is in love with Lord Byron. Byron was at breakfast and spoke highly of Septimus and his article making fun of Chater's previous work; Chater heard the comment.

Thomasina reasons that if there are equations describing a bell curve, aren't there equations to describe other natural things? Thomasina mourns for the great library of Alexandra where many great works were burned and lost. Septimus argues that, throughout history, works are never truly lost, but reappear later.

Chater and Brice enter, with Chater again wanting to challenge Septimus. Lady Croom makes her entrance and requests a copy of *The Couch of Eros* for Lord Byron to include in his book, *English Bards and Scotch Reviewers*. Chater rightly concludes that Byron means to insult him. Lady Croom sees Septimus' copy of Chater's book and borrows it for Byron. Septimus, left alone with Brice and Chater declares that he'd like to kill the poet and plans a gun duel for five o'clock the next morning, with the Brice duel five minutes after the first. Septimus muses upon the outcome of the duels, expecting his two rivals will be dead, and he will leave the country with Byron becoming Thomasina's tutor.

Scene Four opens with Hannah reading to Valentine from Thomasina's math primer. Thomasina had written iterated algorithms (as Valentine explains, she had fed the answers she computes from her equation into the next equation, endlessly looping the output to the input). Valentine defensively claims that Thomasina was simply playing with numbers and not understanding what she was doing. He does admit, though, that a mathematical equation could describe the shape of a leaf.

Hannah hands Bernard a letter mentioning that Captain Brice married Mrs. Chater. Bernard takes this as evidence that his hypothesis is correct: Byron killed Mr. Chater in a duel. Hannah feels that his case isn't proven. Valentine says that Byron's name is recorded in his family's game book as having shot a hare and tells Hannah that Thomasina was hindered by the lack of a computer. A computer does iterated algorithms in seconds, but the long-hand written method would take thousands of pages and lots of time.

Act Two (Scene Five) opens with Bernard reading his lecture notes to Valentine, Chloë and Gus. He is laying out his arguments for Chater's death at Byron's hand when Hannah bursts in. He cites as evidence the three letters which were among the leaves of the *The Couch of Eros* that Byron had borrowed from Septimus Hodge, and was in his possession when that copy of the book was sold in 1816. Hannah challenges each of Bernard's assumptions, upsetting him. Hannah, exasperated, tells Bernard he's greedy and jumping to conclusions that will cause him embarrassment. Valentine, Chloë and Gus run out of the room, and Hannah and Bernard are left to argue about an illustration of Lord Byron and Caroline Lamb that supposedly appears in the book. Hannah feels on instinct alone that it is the poet and his lover; Bernard disagrees.

Bernard suddenly asks Hannah to go with him to London for sex; she declines. After London and the lecture, Bernard is returning to Sidley Park to accompany Chloë to the party. Bernard hands Hannah a book from 1832 that mentions that a hermit, living in the hermitage with his pet tortoise, discovered the second law of thermodynamics. From this and other evidence, Hannah concludes the hermit was Septimus.

At the start of Scene Six, it's dawn on the day of the duel. Septimus comes inside with two pistols and gives a dead rabbit to Jellaby (for the rabbit pie that Thomasina likes). Jellaby tells him that a carriage bore away Captain Brice, Mr. Chater and Mrs. Chater in the early morning and Byron left by horse. Lady Croom found Mrs. Chater leaving Lord Byron's room in the night. Septimus asks if Byron left the book that he had borrowed. Lady Croom enters, dismisses Jellaby to prepare her infusion and throws two opened letters on the table.

Septimus had written an explicit love letter to her and a letter about rice pudding to Thomasina in case of his death by duel. Lady Croom says that she has sent the others away. Jellaby re-enters with the infusion and brings a letter that Byron left for Septimus, which he burns without reading. Lady Croom tells Septimus that Captain Brice and the Chaters are in the Indies; her brother has taken Mrs. Chater as his mistress and Mr. Chater is plant-gathering.

Lady Croom muses that passion is often directed everywhere but where it's supposed to be. Lady Croom feels deceived that Septimus made love to Mrs. Chater when she is the one who received the love note from him. He replies that in the throes of unrelieved passion, he could imagine he was making love to her Ladyship. She tells him to meet her in her sitting room at seven o'clock with a book. He proceeds to burn the two letters.

For Scene Seven, the final scene, the two time periods overlap—there are no distinguishing breaks between the past and the present. Valentine, Chloë and Gus are in Regency period costume. Chloë reads from two Saturday newspapers, which talk about Bernard's Byron/Sidley Park connection. Chloë muses that the future is pre-programmed, but the only thing making it unpredictable is sex and people experiencing passion for those not in the plan. It's the attraction that Newton didn't account for in his laws.

Thomasina shows Septimus that she has run out of paper for doing her equations; Valentine shows Hannah the pattern emerging from pushing Thomasina's equation through the computer millions of times. Valentine points out that Hannah's tea will only go to room temperature on its own; it won't get hot again. In other words, the scientific equation only works one way.

According to Thomasina, Septimus promised to teach her to waltz and sealed the pact with a kiss. Septimus reveals that someone in Paris has found a contradiction of the law of Newton, similar to the mathematical equations Thomasina had been working on. The sound of piano-playing is heard next door, and Thomasina says that her mother is falling in love with Count Zelinsky, who plays the piano with her. Septimus becomes agitated.

Lady Croom enters and complains about the monotonous noise of Mr. Noakes' Newtonian steam engine. Newton's determinism is thrown by the action of bodies in heat, says Thomasina. Her mother further complains about the everpresent mud where garden used to be and asks about the cowshed. Hermitage, Noakes corrects.

Augustus asks if Septimus has an older brother. Yes, Septimus replies, his older brother is the editor of the *Piccadilly Recreation*. Hannah reads and tells Bernard that the dwarf dahlia was discovered by the same Chater who was at Sidley Park and died of a monkey bite in Martinique. It would render Bernard's theory wrong, since Chater would not have died in a duel with Byron. Hannah says that she'll write a letter to the *Times* tomorrow, clueing them into her discovery. The assembled, minus Hannah, leave to have their photo taken in Regency period clothes.

Thomasina tries to coerce Septimus to teach her to waltz. Septimus continues to read her essay, which Valentine and Hannah recognize in their time as the diagram for heat exchange. As Septimus observes, "[t]he Improved Newtonian

Universe must cease and grow cold." In light of the discovery, Thomasina and Septimus dance. The dance is bittersweet, because the audience senses that Thomasina has fallen in love with Septimus (and probably he with her), and she is destined to die in a fire tonight. Septimus kisses Thomasina, but he turns down the invitation to her room. Chloë and Bernard are caught having sex in the hermitage by Lady Croom and Bernard leaves quickly. Gus presents Hannah with a drawing Thomasina had done of Septimus with his tortoise—a tortoise being associated with the hermit—proving Hannah's theory that Septimus becomes the hermit who continues to iterate Thomasina's equations after her death. Gus and Hannah begin to dance awkwardly. Septimus and Thomasina continue their fluid dancing to end the play.

LIST OF CHARACTERS IN

Arcadia

1809/1812 CHARACTERS

Thomasina Coverly, shown in the play at ages 13 and 16, is a bright, questioning, budding scientist who discovers that, unlike Newtonian equations, there are equations that only run one-way (the Second Law of Thermodynamics). Although everyone around her, particularly Septimus and her mother, try to safekeep her innocent naïveté, she is much more insightful than they realize. With a sense of humor and calmness regarding her discovery that the world is "doomed," she eventually falls in love with her tutor Septimus.

Septimus Hodge is Thomasina's twenty-two year old (later, twenty-five) tutor who is caught "in carnal embrace" with Mrs. Chater, but it is Lady Croom he loves from afar. He's clever (insulting Ezra Chater's poetry without him knowing it and sleeping with his wife without repercussion) and book-smart (keeping up with Thomasina intellectually)—and knows it. His self-assurance borders on the arrogant. In a bittersweet moment, he teaches Thomasina to waltz and kisses her, but turns down the invitation to her room. In the end, he becomes the hermit of Sidley Park, filling pages with equations and trying to disprove Thomasina's conclusion of doom.

Lady Croom, in her middle thirties, is Thomasina's mother and the lady of Sidley Park. Her husband is often out hunting. She is not immune to love, as she is as entranced by Lord Byron (and later, a Polish count), as Septimus is by her. She's a bit imperious, bending the inhabitants and guests to her will, telling them that things are as she says in her house. Her vulnerability shows when she catches Mrs. Chater at the door of Lord Byron's room; hurt by their actions, she banishes them. She eventually softens to Septimus' affections and invites him to her room.

Augustus Coverly, Thomasina's fifteen-year-old brother, is haughty and overbearing, probably as a result of his schooling at Eton. Near the end of the play, he asks Septimus to answer his questions about sex.

Mrs. Chater is the adulterous wife of Ezra Chater and a character who exists "off-stage." She has affairs with several of Sidley Park's men, including Septimus, Captain Brice, and probably Lord Byron.

Lord Byron is a much-talked-about, but never-seen character. He is the object of Lady Croom's unrealized passion and Mrs. Chater's probably-realized passion. He's the author of *Childe Harold's Pilgrimage* and a classmate of Septimus'. He is banished from Sidley Park when Mrs. Chater is found at his door. In the present day, Bernard mistakenly credits him with killing Ezra Chater in a duel.

Ezra Chater is a thirty-one year old poet, and a bad one at that. He wrote *The Couch of Eros*, which Septimus travestied in a review. Worse, the man is cuckolded several times, as his wife was involved with Septimus, Captain Brice, and Lord Byron. But he doesn't seem to blame his wife for these dalliances, and is easily fooled into thinking that she slept with Septimus in exchange for a favorable book review. He accompanies Captain Brice and Mrs. Chater—now conducting an open affair—on board a ship to Martinique. Although he discovers a new species of dahlia on the island, he dies rather indecorously of a monkey bite.

Captain Brice, Thomasina's uncle and Lady Croom's brother, is in his middle thirties. His relationship with Mrs. Chater and their journey by boat causes some present-day confusion with regard to Ezra Chater and Lord Byron.

Richard Noakes, a middle-aged landscape architect, is maligned by almost everyone. He discovers Mrs. Chater's indiscretion in the gazebo through his spyglass. His goal, though, is to transform Sidley Park into a picturesque garden, in the style of Salvador Rosa's paintings, an idea somewhat resisted by Lady

Croom. He is responsible, though, for the introduction of the hermitage that becomes the focus of the present-day investigation of the "Sidley Park hermit."

Jellaby, a stereotypical butler, is a middle-aged busybody. Thomasina overhears him telling the cook about the couple caught in "carnal embrace."

PRESENT-DAY CHARACTERS

Hannah Jarvis, is an author in her late thirties. She is researching the Sidley Park hermit, seeing him as a symbol of "the decline from thinking to feeling." With her classical reserve, she isolates herself, not wanting to be involved with sex or love, although she has ample opportunity. Ironically, her published book was about love, as it chronicled the love affair between Lady Carolyn Lamb and Lord Byron. Her scholarship is more thorough and accurate than Bernard's. She doesn't tend to jump to conclusions as he does. Significantly, she delights in proving Bernard wrong about the connection between Ezra Chater and Lord Byron and threatens to inform the newspapers herself.

Bernard Nightingale, a don in his late thirties, is a sloppy scholar, more interested in fame than in historical accuracy. He arrives at Sidley Park in outlandish attire, cleverly lying about his identity when he talks to Hannah Jarvis, whose book he criticized in a review. He needs Hannah to help his investigation of the connection between Ezra Chater and Lord Byron. He concludes hastily that Lord Byron killed Ezra Chater and left the country, explaining Byron's heretofore mysterious departure from England. He is pleased with himself and his "discovery," and prepares to share his findings with the world. Already envisioning his fame, he conceitedly dismisses any questions or challenges put to him. He is crushed when he is ultimately proven wrong. In the course of his investigations, he propositioned Hannah for sex, but she turned him down. He sleeps instead with the half-his-age Chloë and leaves Sidley Park when they are discovered mid-act by her mother.

Valentine Coverly, Chloë and Gus' twenty-five then thirty-year-old brother, is getting his doctorate from Oxford in biology. He helps Hannah understand Thomasina's brilliant discoveries by explaining feedback loops and population dynamics. He reacts first with disbelief, then with grudging admiration for the earlier Coverly. Without the benefit of a computer, he judges Thomasina's efforts to border on insanity. As he works with Hannah, he falls for her and tells her that they're "engaged."

Chloë Coverly, the eighteen-year-old sister of Valentine and Gus Coverly, is preoccupied with sex. She is infatuated with Bernard, has sex with him, and is hurt when he doesn't take the encounter seriously. She is insightful enough, though, to recognize that sex is chaotic: "... because of sex ... The universe is deterministic all right, just like Newton said ... but the only thing going wrong is people fancying people who aren't supposed to be in that part of the plan."

Gus Coverly is Valentine and Chloë's fifteen-year-old brother. He's always silent, but his family calls him a genius. In fact, he was able to help his archaeologist mother find the correct place to start digging when experts had steered her wrong. He's secretly in love with Hannah, as his brother seems to realize.

CRITICAL VIEWS ON
Arcadia

DEREK B. ALWES ON THE PLAY AS A COMEDY

[Derek B. Alwes is an Assistant Professor in the English Department at Ohio State University's Newark campus, where he teaches British literature, particularly the English Renaissance. The subjects of his published articles have included Spenser, Greene, Lyly, and Toni Morrison. In this excerpt, he argues that the audience is given "a godlike perspective" on the play that leads to an interpretation of *Arcadia*'s last scene as a beginning, not an ending; therefore, the play can be classified as a comedy.]

In the final scene of the play, two couples—one from each time period—are waltzing. The modern day couple, Hannah and Gus, are described as waltzing "awkwardly," while Septimus and Thomasina waltz "fluently" (97, stage directions). The contrast between the two could be interpreted as evidence of decline, as evidence of the Second Law of Thermodynamics operating in human civilization. To do so, however, would be to see the play as a tragedy. The charming and brilliant Thomasina is about to go upstairs to bed where *we* know she will die in a fire. If that is all we can think about as the curtain falls, we have missed the play's most important message.[9] If, on the other hand, we have been paying attention to all the clues, the play has prepared us to accept the implications of the simultaneity of the final scene. We are not looking at evidence of loss or decline over time; we are not even looking at "time." We are looking at the human condition. The Dance. It embraces beginnings and ends, creation and loss, life and death—simultaneously. The insights that our privileged, godlike perspective has conferred on us are not finally limited to the vicarious pleasure we take in the brilliant and passionate lives of these fictional characters, because the primary effect on the audience is not a result of the dramatic action itself but of the experience of our expanded perspective.

The perspective we gain is on our own lives as timebound creatures. As Bernard says, "If knowledge isn't self-knowledge it isn't doing much, mate." (61).

Stoppard's *Arcadia* is not a tragedy; it is a comedy. It may be useful to think of the term as it occurs in Dante's *Divine Comedy* rather than in modern "sitcoms," since the laughter, which is frequent, is almost always deepened by an awareness of mortality, but the larger perspective conferred on us as audience takes the sting out of the individual instances of suffering and loss, and the final resolution is hopeful, and hence comic.[10] The crucial difference between Stoppard's comic resolution and Dante's is that Stoppard rejects any eschatological escape from the human condition. For Hannah, human worth is defined not by eschatology but by epistemology: "It's wanting to know that makes us matter. Otherwise we're going out the way we came in" (75). She goes on to explicitly repudiate an *afterlife*:

> That's why you can't believe in the afterlife, Valentine. Believe in the after, by all means, but not the life. Believe in God, the soul, the spirit, the infinite, believe in angels if you like, but not in the great celestial get-together for an exchange of views. If the answers are in the back of the book I can wait, but what a drag. Better to struggle on knowing that failure is final. (75–76)

Instead of a heavenly "afterlife" among the angels, Stoppard's play offers a vision of mortal life extended, through virtually infinite time.

> Hannah: Do you mean the world is saved after all?
> Valentine: No, it's still doomed. But if this is how it started, perhaps it's how *the next one* will come. (78, emphasis added)

As the universe cools, the energy it gives off is not "lost"—as Valentine says, "The heat goes into the mix" (94). According to current theory, the universe, which is now expanding, will collapse upon itself in time, ultimately generating another "big bang and beginning itself anew. That new universe will not, of course, be identical to this one, but perhaps the things that matter to us, the things that make this world so loved, will be recreated. Perhaps the plays of Sophocles (and even the plays of Stoppard) will be "written again in another language."

The rebirth of worlds is an appropriate metaphor for theatrical productions. The play that ends today with dancing and the threat of impending tragic death opens again tomorrow with a "carnal embrace." Thomasina will return to charm us again, and the researchers will again retrieve bits of the beloved past, and the self-contained dramatic universe will unfold under the watchful eyes of loving "gods." The play's existentialist emphasis on the human "struggle," however, reminds us that our privileged god's-eye view is only temporary. When we leave the theater, time begins again for us. As I have already suggested, though, even the temporary experience of this larger perspective on human events can be consoling because it makes loss, even tragic loss, less devastating. In the face of the Second Law of Thermodynamics and its prediction of the ultimate death of the universe, it is difficult to escape the conclusion that "It's *all* trivial" (75), but the play's constant reminders of the creative capacity of the human spirit offer the profound consolation that human endeavors "matter," that it is all "worth it," after all. Perhaps it is Stoppard's own godlike perspective as a creator of worlds that enables him to share that perspective with us.

NOTES

9. Hynes, who argues that *Arcadia* is not generically a comedy because it lacks a comic resolution, says that our knowledge of the impending death of Thomasina at the end of the play "crushes us" (653).

10. Stoppard achieves a very similar effect (though the final resolution may be less hopeful) in his earlier work *Rosencrantz and Guildenstern Are Dead*, in which the confusion and distress of the two central characters are comical to the audience whose perspective includes a knowledge of the larger play, the larger "universe," involved.

—Derek B. Alwes, "'Oh, Phooey to Death!': Boethian Consolation in Tom Stoppard's *Arcadia*." *Papers on Language & Literature* 36, 4 (2000): pp. 401–403.

Paul Edwards on the Role of the Second Law of Thermodynamics

[Paul Edwards, who teaches English at Bath Spa University College and has published and edited works on Wyndham Lewis, comments on the ways that the play uses irreversible, one-way processes—such as translation, time, heat, and fire—to illustrate the theme of the Second Law of Thermodynamics and to show that these processes end in chaos.]

He [Septimus] has set Thomasina a passage in Latin to translate into English. Unknown to her, it is a Latin version of Enobarbus' speech from *Antony and Cleopatra* (2.2, ii, 191ff.), describing Cleopatra, "The barge she sat in, like a burnish'd throne," etc. Here is a great work "written again in another language." Thomasina's stumbling version proves that translation is a one-way process, and that what is once lost remains lost. Classical, "optimistic" cosmology fails to take account of this. *Arcadia* is full of instances that confirm the irreversibility of time. Stoppard is careful to specify that certain props (books, folders) that appear in both time frames of the play should exist in both "new" and "worn" versions. The garden is changed, game is slaughtered. Letters by Byron and Septimus are burnt and reduced to ash. Candles and oil lamps burn. Most poignantly of all, we learn from a retrospective comment of Hannah's in the final scene, Thomasina herself will be burnt to death on the eve of her seventeenth birthday in an accident presumably involving a candle: "et in Arcadia ego" indeed. This final scene is a brilliant example of Stoppard's stagecraft, in which the two periods of time merge as the audience see superimposed on each other, as it were, the actions of 1993 and 1812 (just before Thomasina's seventeenth birthday and her death, thus three years later than the earlier scenes). Thomasina will not die, however, until she has made various anachronistic discoveries and observations. In the 1809 scenes she has puzzled over the fact that jam stirred into her rice pudding cannot be "unstirred" out of it by reversing the movement of her spoon. This is not a particularly radical observation itself, of course, but Thomasina, unlike Septimus at this stage, realizes some of its importance; perhaps God is not a "Newtonian," she suggests. Valentine explains the science of this to Hannah when she is beginning to suspect, from examining Thomasina's surviving exercise book, that she may have been a genius who anticipated later scientific and mathematical discoveries. Valentine's example is of a cup of tea that gradually cools to room temperature: Thomasina's jam disperses into the rice pudding like the heat of the tea into the surrounding atmosphere. Thomasina has made an intuitive discovery of the second law of thermodynamics, which was not formulated until 1865 by the German physicist Rudolf Clausius, the inventor of the term "entropy" to refer to the quantification of the dispersal of heat into its surroundings. Although the first law of thermodynamics announces the "Newtonian" fact that the energy of the universe is constant (nothing, therefore, is lost, just as Septimus had asserted), energy is not always available, for it dissipates into a uniform diffusion and cannot be recovered.

It was at least in part the invention and development of heat engines, particularly steam engines, that led scientists to the second law of thermodynamics. Joseph Fourier's *Analytic Theory of Heat* (1822) and Sadi Carnot's *Reflections on the Motive Power of Fire* (1828) were the necessary precursors to its formulation. In the final scene of *Arcadia*, Noakes, the landscape gardener who has played havoc with Sidley's ideal landscape, brings his "Improved Newcomen steam pump" to the park. Thomasina, casually reading "a prize essay for the Scientific Academy in Paris," immediately perceives that "Newton's equations go forwards and backwards, they do not care which way. But the heat equation cares very much; it goes only one way. That is the reason Mr. Noakes's engine cannot give the power to drive Mr. Noakes's engine" (p. 87). It is also the reason, she implies, why the whole universe must be gradually evening out, in temperature and declining to a state of maximum entropy. Just as Noakes's engine, when its fuel is burnt out, will cease, so the "Improved Newtonian Universe" (p. 93), when all its heat has burnt up, will also cease, except as a randomly distributed mass of irrecoverable energy: chaos. (...)

Stoppard scrupulously has Valentine limit the optimism or meliorism apparently inherent in this overcoming of entropy (the world is "still doomed. But if this is how it started, perhaps it's how the next one will come"; p. 78), but it explains, finally, Hannah's mystery of the mad hermit scribbling thousands of sheets of calculations. It was Septimus Hodge, who begins the play as a "classical" optimist, blithe, witty, and apparently completely imperturbable. Thomasina has shown him the gloomy future implied by the second law of thermodynamics that she has discovered. A contemporary account of the hermit is discovered stating that "Frenchified mathematick ... brought him to the melancholy certitude of a world without light or life ... as a wooden stove that must consume itself until ash and stove are one, and heat is gone from the earth" (p. 65). His "madness" consists in spending twenty-two years reiterating Thomasina's equations after her death, desperate to overturn this pessimistic conviction through restoring pattern and the promise of life in the ocean of ashes. This is "mad" because it can only be done through a computer; the classical Septimus has become his opposite, a full-blooded Romantic (just as, far less affectingly, Hapgood became her temperamental opposite). The truth, the emotional core of this madness, left typically unstated by Stoppard, but all the more poignant for that reason, is that by the eve of Thomasina's seventeenth birthday, Septimus and she are in love, though they are not even aware of it themselves. The pain of her irrecoverable loss in the fire must be at the root of the hermit's desperate attempts to restore hope "through good English algebra" (p. 65).

At the end of the story, after all the researches, and despite entropy, just about everything has been recovered, and, by an irony I have reserved from my discussion of Septimus's earlier speech, "Mathematical discoveries glimpsed [by Thomasina] and lost to view ... have their time again." The final scene of the play shows us an image of perfect harmony, time overcome through the copresence of past and present as the modern couple Hannah and the new, silent genius of the Coverly family, Gus, dance alongside Thomasina and Septimus to the tune of a waltz. But the audience knows that "tomorrow" or "tonight," Thomasina will take a candle, mount the stairs to her bedroom and be burnt to death. She cannot be brought back—certainly not by algebra. The overcoming of time at the conclusion of *Arcadia* is a triumph of art, not of science, and like all such triumphs it is momentary, fragile, and all the more poignant for being quite useless.

—Paul Edwards, "Science in *Hapgood* and *Arcadia*," *The Cambridge Companion to Tom Stoppard*, ed. Katherine E. Kelly, (Cambridge: Cambridge University Press, 2001): pp. 179–180, 182–183.

JOHN FLEMING ON THE SYMBOLISM OF THE CHARACTERS

[John Fleming, the Director of Graduate Studies in the Theatre Department at Southwest Texas State University, divides the characters into two groups: those representing science and those representing arts/humanities. He further discusses how the characters contribute to the play's underlying messages]

In its depiction of people striving to understand the past and to find the keys that unlock the mysteries of nature, *Arcadia* is a celebration of the human struggle to obtain knowledge, with meaning arriving as much out of the process as the product. Also, since Hannah ultimately succeeds in proving her theory and since Thomasina's theories are shown to be accurate, the play is an affirmation that despite all the indeterminacy, people can use their intellect and intuition to gain knowledge. It suggests that science often works, that people can lead fulfilling lives, that even without all the answers, people can be happy, and that interacting with uncertainty is part of what makes human life worth living. Or to paraphrase the theory, life can be chaotic, but also stable, and within chaos there are windows of order.

In the play, Stoppard presents five main characters who are engaged in the quest for knowledge. Thomasina, Septimus, and Valentine are pursuing an understanding of the world from a scientific perspective, while Hannah and Bernard represent the arts and humanities. Characteristic of Stoppard's desire to complicate matters, the three "scientists" are the least Newtonian—Thomasina intuits the shortcomings of the Newtonian model; Septimus is perplexed and made skeptical by her theorems; and Valentine is a working chaotician. In contrast, Hannah and Bernard are more "scientific" in their outlook and approach, and through their respective attempts to interpret the past, Stoppard exhibits classical and romantic temperaments at work.

Hannah's dominant personality is "scientific" and classical in that she is a champion of the dispassionate intellect. Her research on the evolution of the gardens at the Coverly estate is aimed at documenting "the decline from thinking to feeling" (27). To her, the Romantic movement was a "sham," while the ordered, classical garden represented "paradise in the age of reason" (27). Hannah, who sees the world in binary terms, privileges thought over emotion, the classical temperament over the romantic. Disliking sentimentality and limiting her emotional expressions to instances of the gains and losses of the intellect, Hannah views emotion as an unwanted irregularity, a potential collapse into disorder. Ironically, to prove her idea that "The Age of Enlightenment [was] banished into the Romantic wilderness" (66), Hannah must rely on instinct and intuition. In short, she embodies Stoppard's notion that classical and romantic temperaments are not mutually exclusive, but rather coexist in people. Again, it is a matter of life being understood via a both/and paradigm as opposed to an either/or model.

In contrast to Hannah, Bernard embodies the romantic temperament in that he is more energetic, more passionate, and more prone to intuition. Dressed with a flamboyant flair (15), Bernard's character is one of style over substance. Characteristic of a romantic, Bernard takes a fervently intuitive approach to his research: "By which I mean a visceral belief in yourself. Gut instinct. The part of you which doesn't reason. The certainty for which there is no back-reference. Because time is reversed. Tock, tick goes the universe and then recovers itself, but it was enough, you were in there and you bloody *know*" (50). While the laws of the universe indicate that time can only go forward, Bernard's declaration suggests that human intuition is an aspect of life that is more mysterious, something that cannot be confined and explained by science. Typical of Stoppard's complicating of perspectives, Bernard's gut instinct is proved dead wrong, while Hannah is ultimately able to prove the validity of her instinctually derived thesis that Septimus was the hermit of Sidley Park. Thus, human intuition is neither completely valorized nor debunked.

While Bernard's dominant temperament is romantic, he, too, exhibits traits of the scientific and classical personality. When he tries to reconstruct the story of Byron's stay at Sidley Park, he thinks in terms of strict linearity and order. He accumulates data from a variety of sources, and then tries to make it fit his preordained cause-and-effect pattern. He makes the mistake of starting with a desired conclusion, and only seeks information that will make his line of reasoning sufficiently logical. Bernard's unerring faith in his theory makes the lack of convincing evidence immaterial; he is determined to prove his theory whether it is true or not. While Bernard's arrogance and lust for fame are obvious character flaws, his more subtle shortcoming is that his sought-after explanation is based on a Newtonian paradigm of complete order; that is, it ignores the complexity and contradiction of real life, such as the fact that Byron took Septimus's book and that one of Byron's letters was burned. Instead of trying to understand how the events actually occurred, he has created an idealized account. His Newtonian narrative is limited, and ultimately is proved false because Bernard has allowed himself to see only what he has wanted to see. Hannah summarizes the problems of Bernard's approach to scholarship: "You've left out everything which doesn't fit.... You're arrogant, greedy, and reckless. You've gone from a glint in your eye to a sure thing in a hop, skip, and a jump" (59).

While Bernard is the object of Stoppard's satire on the excesses of academic ambition and competition, he is also an advocate for another type of knowledge—the understanding that comes from the appreciation of art. Possessing a romantic temperament, Bernard provides a passionate defense of art, as he argues that art and artistic genius are mysterious realms of life that cannot be quantified in scientific terms: "Parameters! You can't stick Byron's head in your laptop! Genius isn't like your average grouse" (60). Soon Valentine and Bernard argue over what information is and is not worth knowing:

> VALENTINE: But it doesn't matter. Personalities. What matters is the calculus. Scientific progress. Knowledge....
> BERNARD: Why does scientific progress matter more than personalities? ... Don't confuse progress with perfectibility. A great poet is always timely. A great philosopher is an urgent need. There's no rush for Isaac Newton. We were quite happy with Aristotle's cosmos. Personally I preferred it. Fifty-five crystal spheres geared to God's crankshaft is my idea of a satisfying universe. I can't think of anything more trivial than the speed of light. Quarks, quasars—big bangs, black holes—who gives a shit? How did you people con us out of all that status? All that money? (61)

Stoppard notes that Bernard's polemic against science is "a kind of performance art" that "does not speak for me" (Hawkes 268).

The exchange does, however, greatly define the characters, and it articulates different approaches and conceptions of knowledge. Valentine takes a traditional scientific approach in valuing knowledge itself, suggesting that knowledge can be separated from the context that produces it, a view antithetical to most contemporary literary theory. Bernard, on the other hand, offers a romantic valorization of art and philosophy. In part, Bernard suggests that great art is timeless, a view that coincides with his desire for a mechanistic universe; that is, the laws of the Newtonian universe are insensitive to time. The close of Bernard's speech points to the commercialization of knowledge, a theme that flickers in the background of *Arcadia*. Bernard's paradoxical nature is that he wants to prove his theory of Byron not because of any particular literary value it offers, but rather because of the fame and fortune it will bring him. In contrast to this commercialization of knowledge, Bernard follows up his diatribe by saying: "If knowledge isn't self-knowledge it isn't doing much, mate. Is the universe expanding? Is it contracting?

... Leave me out. I can expand my universe without you. [Quotes lines of Byron's poetry]" (61). Here, Bernard takes a knowledge-for-knowledge's-sake approach as he stresses how knowledge, particularly that gained from art, has value for its abstract capacity for enriching human life on a personal, nonutilitarian basis.

—John Fleming, *Stoppard's Theatre: Finding Order Amid Chaos*, Literary Modernism Series, (Austin: University of Texas Press, 2001): pp. 200–205.

HERSH ZEIFMAN ON SEX AND CHAOS

[Hersh Zeifman is Professor of English and Drama at York University in Ontario. He has published articles on contemporary British and American drama in addition to editing *Contemporary British Drama 1970-90* and *David Hare: A Casebook*. In this excerpt, he shows how the play ties together and equates attraction/sex with the scientific principles of Chaos Theory.]

Although Bernard's romanticism is portrayed by Stoppard as deeply (and hilariously) flawed, so too is Hannah's "classical reserve" (p. 75). The problem with Hannah's attempt to inhabit her own private version of "Arcadia," a paradise of rationality and predictability, is that God ultimately is *not* a Newtonian: there is a "serpent" in the garden, and that serpent, as always, is the irrational and seductive power of Eros. At the end of scene 2, the first scene set in the present, Chloë's teenaged brother Gus, who is in love with Hannah, offers her an apple; at the beginning of scene 3, set in the past, the same apple is eaten by Septimus. That iconic apple reminds us simultaneously of Newton's apple (the law of gravity) and the apple with which Eve tempted Adam (the law of desire)—a law of equal gravity that will prove to be the far stronger force. For what finally defeats Newton (and the Newtonian/classical sensibility of Hannah) is, as Thomasina will discover, "The action of bodies in heat" (p. 84). Thomasina is referring here to the physical structure of the universe; what she has stumbled on, long before its time, is thermodynamics, the study of heat that first burned away some of the certainties of Newtonian determinism. But she is also alluding to the action of *human* bodies in heat, the forbidden fruit of Eros.

Stoppard slyly emphasizes this connection between bodies in heat in physics and bodies in heat in the throes of erotic passion in a stage direction in the play's final scene. In the offstage music room, Lady Croom, Thomasina's mother, is playing a romantic piano duet with Count Zelinsky, the latest in her long string of lovers (for Lady Croom, it's not just the heat—it's the tumidity); in the offstage garden, landscape architect "Culpability" Noakes is proudly employing the Improved Newcomen steam pump, a heat engine with which he is reshaping the garden: "*The piano music becomes rapidly more passionate, and then breaks off suddenly in mid-phrase. There is an expressive silence next door which makes* SEPTIMUS *raise his eyes ... The silence allows us to hear the distant regular thump of the steam engine ...*" (p. 81). The sounds of heat collide with the sounds of heat, and the heat of Eros is at least as fatal to Newtonian order as the heat of thermodynamics—as Chloë later suggests in a conversation with her mathematician brother Valentine:

> CHLOË. The universe is deterministic all right, just like Newton said, I mean it's trying to be, but the only thing going wrong is people fancying people who aren't supposed to be in that part of the plan.
> VALENTINE. Ah. The attraction that Newton left out. All the way back to the apple in the garden. (pp. 73–74)

"The attraction that Newton left out" leads inevitably to chaos—and thus to Chaos Theory. For Thomasina similarly manages to discover the science of chaos long before its time: in scene 3 she picks up Hannah's/Septimus's apple (that apple again!) and vows to plot its leaf and deduce its equation, thus anticipating the mathematics of fractals, "the New Geometry of Irregular Forms" (p. 43). "Where chaos begins, classical science stops," writes James Gleick in *Chaos: making a new science*; specifically, Gleick notes, "chaos cuts away at the tenets of Newton's physics" by eliminating the "fantasy of deterministic probability." In the present-day scenes of *Arcadia*, Valentine attempts to explain chaos theory to Hannah:

> The unpredictable and the predetermined unfold together to make everything the way it is ... The ordinary-sized stuff which is our lives, the things people write poetry about—clouds—daffodils—waterfalls—and what happens in a cup of coffee when the cream goes in—these things are full of mystery ... The future is disorder ... It's the best possible time to be alive, when almost everything you thought you knew is wrong. (pp. 47–48)

Poor Hannah—thermodynamics to the left of her, chaos to the right of her, and Eros (which, Hesiod informs us in *Theogony*, is literally Chaos's child) sneaking in behind, all making a mockery of her classical sensibility.

And it gets worse: in a chaotically uncertain world, the only certainty is death—even in Arcadia, as Septimus at one point reminds Thomasina. "Even in Arcadia, there am I!" (p. 13), Septimus quotes, translating and interpreting the tomb inscription "Et in Arcadia Ego" in Poussin's celebrated seventeenth-century painting of the same name. But Thomasina does not need reminding, because she knows something still worse: according to the second law of thermodynamics, which she has intuited, it is the entire universe that is dying, inevitably heading towards an entropic dead end. "Heat goes to cold," Valentine explains to Hannah. "It's a one-way street ... It'll take a while but we're all going to end up at room temperature" (p. 78). Thomasina had grasped this more than a century before: the heat equation, she deduced, "goes only one way" (p. 87). As Stoppard's Rosencrantz acknowledged: "for all the compasses in the world, there's only one direction, and time is its only measure."

"So, we are all doomed!," Septimus is forced to conclude, to which Thomasina replies: "(*Cheerfully*) Yes" (p. 93). That stage direction speaks volumes; despite what she knows, Thomasina refuses to give in to despair. At this moment, however, she is thinking of heat in more than one sense: not just the heat of thermodynamics but the heat of Eros. For she is falling in love with Septimus, and begs him to teach her to waltz—that most romantic of dances. In the remarkable final scene of *Arcadia*, past and present seamlessly, and heartbreakingly, merge: Thomasina's and Valentine's explanations of entropy speak to each other simultaneously across the ages:

> SEPTIMUS. So the Improved Newtonian Universe must cease and grow cold. Dear me.
> VALENTINE. The heat goes into the mix. (*He gestures to indicate the air in the room, in the universe.*)
> THOMASINA. Yes, we must hurry if we are going to dance.
> VALENTINE. And everything is mixing the same way, all the time, irreversibly ...
> SEPTIMUS. Oh, we have time, I think.
> VALENTINE. ... till there's no time left. That's what time means.
> SEPTIMUS. When we have found all the mysteries and lost all the meaning, we will be all alone, on an empty shore.
> THOMASINA. Then we will dance. Is this a waltz?
> (pp. 93–94)

Septimus, alas, is wrong: they do *not* have time—not only cosmically but within their own lifetime. For, as we know from the vantage point of the scenes set in the present, this is the very night that Thomasina will die—ironically enough, in a fire: "Be careful with the flame," Septimus warns as he lights the candlestick that will ultimately lead to her death (p. 96). Eros tragically melts into Thanatos; heat consumes in all possible ways. And yet, what other response is there in a world without predictable pattern or meaning except, as Thomasina suggests, to "dance?"

—Hersh Zeifman, "The Comedy of Eros: Stoppard in Love," *The Cambridge Companion to Tom Stoppard*, ed. Katherine E. Kelly, (Cambridge: Cambridge University Press, 2001): pp. 187–190.

The Invention of Love

The Invention of Love is Stoppard's examination of the intellectual versus the emotional in life. A. E. Housman embodies the duality of head/heart, as he was both a poet and a scholar. He was a classical textual scholar and closeted gay man, who became renown in his lifetime with a collection of poems called *A Shropshire Lad*—but he repressed his heart's desire. In contrast, Oscar Wilde lived by his heart's desires. He was a flamboyant playwright who suffered indignities during his lifetime for having an open homosexual relationship, but whose art has better stood the test of time. The play asks several times, "What will become of you?" We already know the answer, because AEH (Houseman) is crossing the River Styx. Everyone dies, but what will be his or her lasting monument?

As Act One opens, seventy-seven-year-old A. E. Housman (referred to as "AEH") waits to cross the River Styx as Charon the ferryman approaches. Charon was told to pick up a poet and a scholar; AEH informs him that he is both. We also learn that he was a Latin professor at Cambridge. AEH may actually be dead and on his way to the underworld, or perhaps he is only dreaming, asleep in his bed at the Evelyn Nursing Home.

In the next scene, the audience is taken back to Houseman's youth. Three university students—Housman (AEH as a young man), Alfred Pollard and Moses "Mo" Jackson—are in a rowboat. The dead Housman watches the younger version of himself in the boat and fondly recalls his best friend, Mo Jackson, saying that he would have died for him, but never had the luck. The scene shifts to the meeting of the three young men in college. Jackson is established as the athlete of the group, while Pollard and and Housman study classics. All three friends complain about the teaching and speak of Catullus as the inventor of the love poem.

Four Oxford professors—Pattison, Jowett, Pater and Ruskin—discuss their educational and sexual morality philosophies over a croquet game. Pattison leaves and Pater flirts with a male Balliol College student. Jowett notices and disapproves; he disagrees with the "Aesthete movement" (code words, of sorts, for "homosexuality").

The three friends, rowing their boat, share thoughts on love poetry. Housman and Pollard both favor Catullus' love poems, while Mo is only interested in such poetry as a means to woo a woman. They continue to ponder the origin of the love poem.

The dons' croquet match continues and Pattison laments Oxford has become overbuilt; he equates Paddington station and modernization with hell. Pattison reaffirms that the University is for predetermined course of scholarly study, not education. Ruskin prefers to instill his students with a love of manual labor.

Housman has been steadily following Jackson's rowing race with Pollard and gossiping about their fellow classmate, Oscar Wilde.

The scene shifts back to the croquet match. Jowett is particularly proud of his role in creating an educated class that fills civil service jobs, while Pattison decries the reduction of Oxford to mediocrity. Jowett champions classical antiquity as the ideal foundation of modern education—as both he and Ruskin agree… "[b]uggery apart." Ruskin supports the Medieval Gothic as the ideal, while Pater proclaims Italy as the start of the Aesthete spirit.

At the end of the race, Jackson tells them a fellow he assumes is an Aesthete complimented him on his left leg. (The fellow, it turns out, was Oscar Wilde).

Pater expounds on the Renaissance as the ideal for teaching how to live for the moment. And, just then, Jowett asks Pater for a "moment."

Jackson runs in the distance and Housman was supposed to be timing him. Instead, he's been watching him.

Jowett criticizes Pater for his correspondence with the young male Balliol student. Pater attempts to defend himself by citing Greek precedent for male love, saying that every other element of that society was venerated. The student has been dismissed, Jowett tells Pater.

Housman and Jowett speak about venerated Latin texts and the corruption that they may suffer after centuries of re-copying.

Robinson Ellis interrupts them, childlike, and defends his somewhat shoddy scholarship in not recognizing the importance of an Oxford Catullus work. Ellis introduces Housman to Propertius, the most corrupt Latin writer. Propertius becomes Housman's long-time scholarly project and part of his legacy.

Charon and AEH arrive at a riverbank. Housman steps ashore and comes face-to-face with the younger version of himself. They enter into conversation about the classics and AEH challenges his younger self to think about the scientists as possibly being superior in regard to sense, morality, taste, etc.— in effect, guiding himself on his life's path. They discuss Propertius and AEH declares that his edition on Propertius was to be the definitive one. Housman wonders how he will leave his mark, and AEH asks if it will be as a poet or a scholar, since he argues that one can't be a first-rank poet, as it will hurt scholarship and vice-versa. Finding errors, such as in texts with misplaced commas—making sense where there formerly was none—is a victory of knowledge, much like science. Housman, still not recognizing his older self, rejoins his two friends and announces that he will become a Latin textual critic, a "scientist" like Jackson.

AEH imagines himself in front of his class, trying to rally his students to appreciate poetry, like Horace's description of Ligurinus, the young athlete running across the Fields of Mars.

Some time has passed at the beginning of Act Two. Housman, now a few years older, and his sister Kate, survey the lands surrounding their home from an overlooking hill. Kate admires her brother's intellect but can't understand why he's failed his university exams. He will become a Civil Servant and mentions that Jackson works at the Patent Office. Housman tells her that he's stopped believing in God and heaven as punishment for his mother's death.

Moving ahead in time a bit more, Housman and Jackson wait for the train in their work clothes. It is apparent in the *Journal of Philology* that Housman holds and the evening paper that Jackson holds that their interests have diverged since the university. Housman now works in the Trade Marks office. Jackson is surprised at this turn of events—Housman had the best potential, but it was Pollard who is rewarded the plum classics job. It's apparent, though, that Housman has taken the job with Jackson to be closer to him. Housman shows Jackson the article he published in the *Journal of Philology* that corrects some of Horace's writings, although his real interest is Propertius. Jackson starts to question the use of the classical philosophers when electricity seems so much more useful. Jackson also starts complaining that Oscar Wilde isn't manly. It is clear from this context that they had seen a play together (*Patience*) that satirized the Aesthete movement and Jackson chose to comment on its electric lighting, concentration on the production rather than the content.

The scene changes and three journalists—Labouchere, Harris, and Stead—are in a room, upset that they as journalists bolstered Oscar Wilde but he's now grown beyond their power to manage him. Labouchere, who also is a Liberal Member of Parliament, stated that he had sent a bill through the House that gives gay men behind closed doors a two-year sentence. He had meant it to be absurd, but it passed. Harris says he was in Greece when the graves of the Sacred Band of Thebes (the army of male lovers) was unearthed.

Chamberlain and Housman are spectators at Jackson's athletics match. Housman is concerned that he can't see Jackson. Chamberlain knows that Housman wants to be "brothers-in-arms" with Jackson and to die for him. Jackson wins his race; Pollard arrives, but has missed the winning moment. Chamberlain leaves, saying he has to meet someone.

Pollard produces the draft of Propertius which Housman gave him, but demurs from making too many comments, since he's not a Propertius scholar. Pollard says that Housman wants a monument, to which Housman replies, "Oh, you've guessed my secret," paralleling a statement made by Chamberlain moments earlier and implying that he is gay like Chamberlain.

In their apartment, Jackson mentions to Housman that his girlfriend Rosa suspects Housman is "sweet on" him, a charge he dismissed (as did Housman). Jackson warns Housman that Chamberlain is gay and getting too close to him may be misunderstood. Housman outs himself by saying that he wants to live close to Jackson and implies Rosa was right about his feelings. Jackson never suspected, saying that Housman is not an Aesthete type. Housman confesses that Jackson is half of his life. Jackson is initially angry, but says, "It's terrible but it's not your fault.... We'll be just like before." They shake hands and Jackson tells him that he thinks Housman will "meet the right girl."

Housman is heartbroken after the handshake. The scene changes and AEH is at a desk as a Selection Committee considers his application for a post at the University. Postgate suggested the appointment, calling him "very likely the best classical scholar in England." AEH gets the job.

Postgate leaves and Stead, Labouchere and Harris discuss Oscar Wilde's two-year sentence under Labouchere's Amendment clause for "indecency between men." Stead asserts he wouldn't have been charged if he had been caught with young virgins instead.

Chamberlain, Harris and Jerome row past Oscar Wilde's place of incarceration. Jerome had a hand in exposing Oscar Wilde in the newspaper. In his view, the wholesome humor of Shakespeare and other dramatists will outlast Wilde's decadent writings. The conversation wanders to Housman's book of poetry, *A Shropshire Lad* and Chamberlain marvels that Housman has become a renowned poet.

Chamberlain says Housman is a Latin professor and Jerome slyly remarks that Housman is "of the Greek persuasion." They compare his manner of dress to Chamberlain's, implying that he, too, is gay.

AEH and Chamberlain talk alone on Jubilee Night, 1897. Chamberlain can't believe that AEH lived to an old age because he was always so unhappy about Jackson. At least he was able to write poems as a result, he says. Chamberlain asks if he ever sent the poems that weren't published to Jackson; Housman says no. Chamberlain admits that he now belongs to a club of men who have labeled themselves 'homosexuals.' AEH thinks the name's terrible because it's half Greek and half Latin.

The scene shifts and Oscar Wilde is reading from *A Shropshire Lad*. Oscar tells AEH that truth has more to do with imagination and art. AEH reveals he dedicated his work on Manilius to

Jackson. A boatman comes to pick up Wilde. AEH tells Wilde that he lived in the wrong age. Wilde reprimands AEH for his silence, his sullenness and his shame. Wilde considers himself to be the artist, pushing the envelope and an agent of change. Wilde asks where AEH has been during this change, to which AEH replies that he has been at home. The boatman pulls away from shore with Wilde.

AEH runs into himself at a younger age and schools himself on the inventor of the love elegy. Not Propertius, as Housman supposes, but Cornelius Gallus, a man whom Virgil wrote of but of whose work only one line survived. Housman, in a scene that's replayed, is called away by his friends Pollard and Jackson in a boat. Jerome K. Jerome, author of *Three Men in a Boat*, wrote in an Oxford magazine that the University was advocating an "unnatural disease." Oscar Wilde had previously written some poems to a male student, but it was Jerome's letter which set off the events leading to Wilde's arrest.

Charon takes Wilde across the Styx. AEH calls it the Golden Age of Oxford with oppositions of the new Christians and new pagans, the hairshirts and the Aesthetes. He feels lucky to be on the shore.

LIST OF CHARACTERS IN
The Invention of Love

AEH, the seventy-seven-year-old, nearly-dying version of A. E. Housman, is given the chance to look back on his life. His body, we learn, may still be in the Evelyn Nursing Home and that this "looking back" is a dream. Somewhat gruff and jaded by his experiences, he visits his younger self and expresses his regrets. Though he was well regarded as a Latin textual scholar and known for his keen intellect, he had repressed his true self. Denying his homosexual attraction and love for his heterosexual classmate, Mo Jackson, Housman poured his emotions into his poetry (*A Shropshire Lad*) rather than disclose them in his real life. Ever the scholar, Housman confesses to his younger self that he regrets failing his Oxford Classics examination and completing his edition of Propertius. As he looks back on himself as a teacher, we see him as passionate about love poems, particularly Horace's poem about Ligurinus, a young athlete, running across the Fields of Mars. Mo is visually equated with Ligurinus, running in the distance, but never getting closer. While he may idealize male love, he chooses not to explore it, except to immortalize Jackson in poetry. He even derides the word "homosexual," saying it mixes Greek with Latin. He admits that his life was "marked by long silences" and Oscar Wilde chastises him for his timidity.

Housman is the younger (ages 18-26) version of A. E. Housman. A Classics student at Oxford, he decides that he will be a Latin textual critic, and will, in effect, be a scientist like Jackson. His failure to pass his exams puts a crimp in his immediate plans and he tells his sister Kate that he will take the civil service exam, presumably so he could work close to Jackson. He confides to Kate that he no longer believes in God as punishment for his mother's death. Although he obtains a job as a patent office clerk, his continuing scholarship eventually garners him an appointment at the University.

Moses John Jackson a.k.a. "Mo" (ages 19-27) is an athlete and sciences student at Oxford with Housman. He is also the object of Housman's unrequited affection. It's clear from his response to Oscar Wilde's flirtation that Mo is heterosexual, even calling Wilde an "Aesthete." His is critical of Wilde and the other Aesthetes and later believes them to be useless and unmanly. Mo, even when presented with his girlfriend's suspicions that Housman is "sweet on him," disbelieves it. When he realizes she was right, he shakes Housman's hand and resolves to be friends, but he feels uncomfortable with the situation. Perhaps Mo isn't very "deep;" after seeing a performance of Gilbert and Sullivan's *Patience*, he can only talk about the theater's lighting. And perhaps insensitively, he questions Housman's contentment in his job as a patent office clerk.

Alfred William Pollard, the third of the Oxford trio of friends, is often seen with Housman and Jackson in a boat with a dog. He, like Housman, studies Classics, but he settles for working in the British Museum. He and Housman joke about Classical scholarship, but he thinks that perhaps Housman's handling of previous scholars borders on disrespect.

Charon is the ferryman of the Underworld who stands by to take Housman across the River Styx. He is supposed to pick up a poet and a scholar, and AEH realizes that they both refer to him. AEH is excited when Charon claims that he can remember lines from lost plays of Aeschylus, but he's disappointed when the boatman can only remember paraphrased snatches of text. Charon also transports Oscar Wilde.

Mark Pattison, sixty-four-year-old Rector of Lincoln College and a classical scholar, ironically dismisses the love of learning and later says the University is meant for predetermined scholarship, not education. He bemoans Oxford as an "overbuilt slum."

Walter Pater, a thirty-eight-year-old critic, essayist, scholar, and fellow of Brasenose College, is an unhandsome dandy who flirts with a young, male Balliol College student. He views the Italian Renaissance as the ideal model for society, encouraging a lifestyle of "living for the moment." Pater, when reprimanded by Jowett for corresponding with a young student, turns Jowett's ideal back on him, defending himself by saying that Greek society, which is venerated, also had love between men.

John Ruskin, fifty-eight-year-old art critic, wants his students to have a love for manual labor. He idealizes Medieval Gothic times as the model for society. His vision of "hell" is Paddington station and as "modernization infinitely expanded."

Benjamin Jowett, who at age sixty is the Master of Balliol and observes Pater flirting with the young Balliol College student. He disagrees with the Aesthetes and their admiration of male beauty. Jowett feels proud of his contributions to creating an educated class of civil servants. He favors a society built on classical Greek and Roman foundations, but without their acceptance of homosexuality. He reprimands Pater for his correspondence with the young student and informs him that the student has been dismissed, a direct result of his actions. In his edition of Phaedrus, he changed all references to homosexuality.

Katherine "Kate" Housman, Housman's sister (ages 19 and 35), clearly feels inferior to Housman's intellect and calls herself a "dunce." Still, she can't understand what happened to her brother academically. She is proud of her brother, though, and realizes that he has a heart after the publication of *A Shropshire Lad*.

Robinson Ellis, whom AEH describes as an "idiot child," is a 45-year-old Latin scholar who appears onstage (on one occasion) with a lollipop and a scooter.

Henry Labouchere, Liberal MP and journalist, ages 54 and 64. He complains that Oscar Wilde was boosted by journalism, then grew beyond their influence. As a member of Parliament, Labouchere introduced the Criminal Law Amendment Act, an unrelated add-on to a proposed bill that would sentence gay men to two years of hard labor. He thought the Amendment was absurd and would be rejected by right-thinking people; now that it's been passed, he feels that it will do more harm than good.

Frank Harris, journalist and writer, ages 29 and about 40. An editor at the *Evening News*, he increased circulation by editing it as if he were a fourteen-year-old. He continually lies about or exaggerates his accomplishments on everything else.

W. T. Stead, editor and journalist, ages 36 and 46, claims that Wilde's relations with men are grossly indecent. The other journalists deem him "mad," as he ate a mouse to see what it tastes like. To increase his paper's circulation, he bought a thirteen-year-old virgin for five pounds "to prove a point" and "invented New Journalism," incorporating interviews, illustrations, and other elements into his newspaper.

Chamberlain, a gay clerk in his 20s, then 30s, "outs" himself to Housman. He realizes that Housman loves Jackson, but tries to tell Housman that such love will only lead to unhappiness because Jackson will not reciprocate. He observes that he wasn't sure if Housman would survive his depression after Mo's marriage. He identifies himself with the label "homosexual."

John Percival Postgate, a Latin scholar, about 40, recommends AEH/Housman's appointment to the University and calls him England's foremost classical scholar. AEH, however, does not agree with Postgate's textual criticism of Prospertius.

Jerome K. Jerome is a mid-thirties humorist and author of *Three Men in a Boat*. As the editor of a popular newspaper, he is indirectly responsible for Oscar Wilde's arrest by his "speaking out" in that public forum, but feels that Wilde's "decadent" work won't last compared to the timeless, wholesome humor of Shakespeare and other playwrights.

Oscar Wilde, age 41, is the famous playwright of *The Importance of Being Earnest* who was jailed for two years for homosexual acts with his lover, Lord Alfred Douglas—"Bosie," as Wilde called him his "poem." Even in his Oxford days, Wilde flirted with Mo Jackson. He is flamboyant and known for it: he throws a Jubilee Day party for fifteen children, complete with cake and chocolates. Despite his jail time and infamy, he doesn't want AEH's sympathy. In fact, he chastises AEH for living his life timidly; he feels that he changed the world and pushed the envelope while AEH was simply at home. Ultimately, he's pleased with his life and his accomplishments.

The Invention of Love

CARRIE RYAN ON TRANSLATING THE PLAY FROM PAGE TO STAGE

[Carrie Ryan, the Literary Manager for La Jolla Playhouse in San Diego and former Literary Manager/Dramaturg for The Wilma Theater in Philadelphia, discusses textual changes that were made to "Americanize" the play for its run at The Wilma Theater.]

In preparing *The Invention of Love* for an American audience, we made a variety of changes to the published text of the play. Director Blanka Zizka began working with Tom Stoppard early in 1999 to shape the text, and I joined their deliberations in the fall as we approached our first rehearsal in January 2000. It was rather inspiring to work with Stoppard on this often tedious process of going over the play line-by-line in order to ensure that our audience would have access to the greater part of its tapestry. He came to the table not as the author of a published, fixed text but as a man of the theater who was interested in, and committed to, making the East Coast premiere of his play as immediate and effective for a Philadelphia audience as the original production had been for a British audience.

Most of the changes we made in the text ultimately were small. The bulk of the play is clear upon close inspection; we found ourselves worried instead about many of the chatty colloquialisms that characters use in the play, idiomatic constructions that could ring foreign in American ears and jolt audience members out of the world we were trying to create. For example, at the play's emotional center, when Housman reveals his feelings to Jackson, the latter confronts Housman about his friendship with a fellow at the Patent Office who is rumored to be gay. After stumbling through his insinuation, Jackson apologizes, "I know I'm all hobnails." Not an idiom used here, and not one whose meaning can be easily divined; the phrase, "all hobnails," we learned from Stoppard, is meant to convey a sort of well-meant clumsiness. In our version, Jackson instead says, "You know I'm all thumbs," a small adjustment that still conveys his awkwardness and good intentions.

Stoppard was particularly interested in adjusting the text when a joke was at stake. In this case, the laughs were not simply for laughs' sake. With a piece as intellectually and emotionally dense as this, each lighter moment becomes all the more important for pace and shape. Nothing draws an audience member into a piece like a joke that comes across, a moment of shared humor that galvanizes actors and audience in a communal journey. One of our worries was that the people in the audience, having heard that the play was centered around a Victorian Classical scholar and poet, would arrive at the theater thinking that they had little in common with this world (which, of course, is not the case since the play presents a fundamentally human rendering of a man's coming to terms with his life's choices). Humor can go a long way toward including an audience, and each joke was an important way of reinforcing the fact that the audience and the characters in the play were sharing the same space and the same journey for three hours in a theater.

Early in the play, AEH says of a fellow Classicist's translation of Sophocles that "the responsibility for reading the metre seems to have been handed over to the Gas, Light and Coke Company" (p. 3). We streamlined this quip, making it simply "Gas Company," a familiar utility. In another example, at the top of Act Two, Housman tells Jackson a story about his job in the Trade Marks Registry. Stoppard had built a joke around a giraffe used to advertise sore throat lozenges, and both director Blanka Zizka and myself had trouble understanding it. The joke as written reads,

I had sore throat lozenges today, an application to register a wonderfully woebegone giraffe—raised rather a subtle point in Trade Marks regulation, actually; it seems there is already a giraffe at large, wearing twelve styles of celluloid collar, but, and here's the nub, a *happy* giraffe, in fact a preening self-satisfied giraffe. The question arises—is the registered giraffe

Platonic?, are all God's giraffes *in esse et in posse* to be rendered unto the Houndsditch Novelty Collar Company? (p. 53)

In this case, it was not the use of Latin but the structure of the joke that gave us pause. We told Stoppard that phrases such as "celluloid collar" were confusing, and that it was not entirely clear to us from the joke as written that both giraffes were being used for advertising. As we explained our confusion, he explained his intention, and we fashioned another version of the joke:

> I had an application today for a wonderfully woebegone giraffe—to advertise lozenges for sore throats, naturally—which, however raised rather a subtle point in Trade Marks regulation, because it seems there is already a giraffe registered to advertise twelve styles of shirt collar. But, and here's the nub, that's a *happy* giraffe. So the question arises—is the registered giraffe Platonic?, are all God's giraffes *in esse et in posse* to be spoken for by the Houndsditch Shirt Collar Company?

Stoppard made no similar change in San Francisco, and while our new version of the joke was on many nights quite funny, Stoppard more than once let us know that the joke as he had written it got laughs from San Francisco audiences.

We simply cut several other Britishisms in the play. The early twentieth-century Oxford that appears in the play is a world unto itself, a university system wherein many elements do not have equivalents in our own system. When Professor Mark Pattison welcomes the boys to Oxford, he says to them, "We have bought you, and we're running you in two plates, Mods and the Finals" (p. 8). Rather than struggling to find some way to explain Mods and Finals through added text, program notes, or acting virtuosity, we chose instead to cut the line. Pattison's cynicism about the Oxford educational system is already well apparent when he says, just a line before this, "if you have come to Oxford with the idea of getting knowledge, you must give that up at once." Housman and his friends later joke about Mods, and we cut that reference as well, along with specific references to rowing at Oxford. England's lower school system has its own jargon as well, so when Housman's sister refers to "Sixth Form"

(p. 50), we substituted simply "class." Again, we were guided in these changes by the pursuit of clarity without sacrificing the spirit and sense of any given moment.

Some further adjustments pertained to the historical figures who populate the play. All of the characters in *The Invention of Love*, save one, are based on actual people who lived, many of whom are more popularly familiar in Britain than they are here. The great Victorian art critic John Ruskin appears in the play, and in the first scene Stoppard establishes a pun at his expense. Charon approaches AEH and asks him to "belay the painter" (p. 1)—that is, to moor his boat to the dock. Making conversation, AEH then says, "I heard Ruskin lecture in my first term at Oxford. Painters belayed on every side" (p. 1). We added the phrase "on art" after "lecture" to help the audience make the connection between Ruskin's academic pursuits and the "painters" whom AEH mentions. Later, Ruskin talks about "an Irish exquisite, a great slab of a youth with white hands and long poetical hair" (p. 15). Since the spectre of Oscar Wilde and his aestheticism runs through the play, we underlined this moment by adding the phrase, "Oscar, they called him," to Ruskin's speech. We wanted whenever possible to reinforce the context of this world and to help the audience place the play's various characters within this context.

One of the changes we made was truly fundamental, affecting the structure of the play. Jerome K. Jerome's novel *Three Men in a Boat* informs the play. When AEH first spies his younger self, Housman is with his friends Jackson and Pollard, rowing on the Thames with a dog in his lap. Much of their dialogue—"Pull on your right, Jackson." "Do you want to take the oars?" "No, you're doing splendidly" (p. 4)—evokes the novel. Late in Act Two, Jerome himself appears in a boat with journalist Frank Harris and Housman's friend Chamberlain (the play's one invented character), and they discuss the fates of both Housman and Oscar Wilde. We worried that Jerome was truly an obscure figure to most Americans; certainly, prior to doing research, no one working on the show knew much about him. Jerome identifies himself in the play as "the editor of a popular newspaper" (p. 85), and immediately prior to his entrance there is a scene featuring the three journalists who appear through Act 2. Why, if Jerome is a journalist, does he not appear in these scenes? For those not familiar with Jerome and his novel, learning that he is a journalist might prove problematic since he is not a part of the scenes with Harris, W. T. Stead, and Henry Labouchère. He appears only once, in one of the play's more dreamlike scenes. Rather than risk alienating the members of our audience so near the end of the play, after they have worked consistently to navigate Greek and Latin in a setting distant in both time and place, we cut the scene in which Jerome appears.

This cut necessitated some reshaping of AEH's penultimate monologue. In it, he explains that Jerome wrote an article that led Lord Alfred "Douglas' father into leaving a card at the Albermarle Club, 'to Oscar Wilde, posing as a Sodomite.' From which all that followed, followed" (p. 101). On a dramaturgical level, the connection between Jerome, whose novel influences the structure of the play, and Wilde, whose aestheticism is posited as an alternative to Housman's choices, is seductive, lifting the dream play from subconscious ramblings to a careful crafted examination of a man's life through the times in which he lived. If the audience does not know Jerome, however, the revelation of this connection can feel more like a lecture than a discovery. For many of the same reasons that we cut the scene in which Jerome appears, we ended up excising his presence from the play entirely. It certainly was not a necessary cut—few of the textual changes which we made were—but we felt, and Stoppard agreed to allow us to try, that the play without Jerome still preserved the essence of the play which Stoppard wrote.

—Carrie Ryan, "Translating *The Invention of Love:* The Journey From Page to Stage For Tom Stoppard's Latest Play." *Journal of Modern Literature* 24, 2 (Winter 2000–2001): pp. 199–201.

JOHN FLEMING ON HOUSMAN VERSUS WILDE

[Here Flemming compares and contrasts A. E. Housman's and Oscar Wilde's approach to life, love, and art.]

Just as the first act interspersed scenes that establish the cultural milieu of Oxford during Housman's undergraduate years, so too Stoppard incorporates scenes that show the social context of London in the late Victorian era, particularly in regard to homosexuality and the Oscar Wilde trials. Stoppard presents the journalists who helped pass the Criminal Law Amendment and the Labouchère Amendment, which made homosexual activity a crime. In the process, Stoppard offers a view of the power, purpose, and peccadilloes of the popular press, a perspective that is both particular to Victorian-era London but that is also partially applicable today. Labouchère laments that the press helped build Wilde's reputation but cannot bring it down. For him, this "shakes one's faith in the operation of a moral universe by journalism" (60). Stead, the stout moralizer who began the crusade to raise the age of consent, believes that "in the right hands the editor's pen is the sceptre of power" (61). He sees his work as a divine mission to dictate public opinion and standards. In contrast, Harris decides to follow public taste and is simply concerned with printing whatever sells, namely sex, violence, and scandal.

The Oscar Wilde trials provided sex and scandal, and the end result was that Wilde was sentenced to two years hard labor and the Aesthetes' cult was driven underground. At the same time as the Wilde trials, the historical Housman composed most of the poems that make up *A Shropshire Lad*. In the play, Chamberlain quotes some of them to AEH; the excerpts often suggest Housman's continuing love for Jackson and the pain of the unrequited lover. Chamberlain also reveals that the word *homosexual* did not enter the English language until 1897. AEH is outraged by the word because, as he says, "It's half Greek and half Latin!" (94). Besides evoking a good laugh, his response is indicative of how Housman dealt with his sexuality; the men who came up with the word were seeking a form of gay identity, an issue relevant to Housman's life, but he responds academically, rather than personally.

This scene then dovetails into AEH's meeting with Wilde, the era's most famous homosexual, and the man whose life serves as a polar opposite to Housman's. Their encounter stands as one of the major thematic moments in the play. Stoppard himself comments: "Wilde was the one who crashed and burned. Housman the one who died a success. But from our standpoint, from 1997, it's Wilde who is the success, and Housman the failure" (T. Hill). More important than the contrast between their reputations is the contrast between how they chose to live their lives.

When AEH meets Wilde the latter is reading a bleak and angry poem from *A Shropshire Lad*, a poem based on a gay man who shot himself after the Wilde trial so as to escape the shame of his homosexuality. Though Wilde is weathered, overweight, and on the decline from his prison experience, he does not share the poet's cynicism. Wilde's passion for life stands in contrast to Housman's reserve. Wilde had friends, Housman had colleagues (97). Wilde moved with the major figures of the era and "lived at the turning point of the world where everything was waking up new," but while all this was going on, Housman was "at home" (100). In part, their lives reflect the divide between the Dionysian and the Apollonian. Wilde lived the sensual, Dionysian life, while Housman opted for the critical-rational mode of the Apollonian. Each man's tragedy resulted from not balancing the two impulses.

Just as the way they lived was different, so too was how they loved. In act I, AEH defines love by quoting Sophocles' *The Loves of Achilles*: "Love feels like the ice held in the hand by children" (44). Stoppard omits Sophocles' explanation of the image: "that however much pleasure the ice gives to start with, the children end up being able neither to hold it nor let it go" (Jones). The explanation, from a play about love between two men, aptly summarizes both Housman's and Wilde's experiences with love: Housman could not hold on to Jackson, while Wilde could never let go of Lord Alfred Douglas, his beloved Bosie.

Wilde posits a difference between facts and truth. What happened is "only fact. Truth is quite another thing and is the work of the imagination" (95–96). He then uses this paradigm to analyze his life and his love for Bosie:

> The betrayal of oneself is lifelong regret. Bosie is what became of me. He is spoiled, vindictive, utterly selfish and

not very talented, but these are merely the facts. The truth is he was Hyacinth when Apollo loved him, he is ivory and gold, from his red rose-leaf lips comes music that fills me with joy, he is the only one who understands me. [Excerpt of love poem], but before Plato could describe love, the loved one had to be invented. We would never love anybody if we could see past our invention. Bosie is my creation, my poem. In the mirror of invention, love discovered itself. Then we saw what we had wrought, rapture and pain together, the ice that burns who clasps it. (98)

Wilde articulates a tendency to idealize the loved one, a process Housman went through with Jackson, inventing the image of his idealized man. The young Housman believes that the Latin poets were "real people in real love," whose writing showed "love as it really is" (102). While those poems are similar to Wilde's notion of the truth, they are still just words on paper, feelings cast into idealized form. They may contain truth, but they are not the same as love experienced. Since Jackson never reciprocated Housman's love, Housman felt the pain of love rejected, but he never fully lived and experienced his idealized love. To his death, he clung to that idealized invention. In contrast, Wilde experienced his idealized love, and discovered that love sometimes involves contrasting passions, both ecstasy and excruciating pain. Wilde and Housman exemplify extremes of love. Wilde knew his love of Bosie would be his destruction, but he felt helpless to resist. Housman was rejected but still clung to his idealized vision of love. In the process he killed off his inner, emotional life as a practical functioning part of his life. In different ways, each man's passion proved fatal.

AEH feels sorry for Wilde, feels that he was a victim of the times: "Your life is a terrible thing. A chronological error. The choice was not always between renunciation and folly" (99). But Wilde asks for no sympathy: "Better a fallen rocket than never a burst of light. Dante reserved a place in his Inferno for those who willfully live in sadness.... Your 'honour' is all shame and timidity and compliance" (99). Rather than see himself as a victim, Wilde suggests that Housman has allowed himself to become a victim of Victorian-era repression. Also, though society may have cut down Wilde in his prime, he will outlive them all: "The blaze of my immolation threw its light into every corner of the land where uncounted men sat each in his own darkness.... I made art a philosophy that can look the twentieth century in the eye. I had genius, brilliancy, daring, I took charge of my own myth" (99–100). Wilde lived fully and openly, and though society imprisoned him for that, he left a legacy that outshines that of the cautious, conservative Housman, who made his own life a prison. Through Wilde, Stoppard expresses a carpe diem theme—that one must be willing to take the risk to seize the day.

In contrast to the ever quotable Wilde, AEH says: "My life is marked by long silences" (98). He admits that he chose a life of solitude, and as AEH looks back on his life, he is filled with melancholy not nostalgia. Before he departs, Wilde expresses his puzzlement over Housman's unhappiness: "You didn't mention your poems. How can you be unhappy when you know you wrote them? They are all that will still matter" (100). Wilde valorizes art as the artist's triumph over life and it is art, not scholarship about art, that endures. While Housman spent more time on his edition of Manilius, it is *A Shropshire Lad* that stands as his monument.

—John Fleming, *Stoppard's Theatre: Finding Order Amid Chaos*, Literary Modernism Series, (Austin, Texas: University of Texas Press, 2001): pp. 239–242.

Hersh Zeifman on Housman's Dualities

[In this excerpt, Zeifman highlights Housman's dualities: scholar (head) and poet (heart), old and young, classical and romantic. In the end, it is Housman's heart that is repressed.]

A. E. Housman, on the other hand, the protagonist of Stoppard's most recent play, *The Invention of Love*, chooses *not* to dance—only to dream of dancing. Once again Stoppard is dramatizing the conflict between a romantic and classical sensibility, but this time within a single character. When asked in an interview in 1998 what originally inspired him to write a play about

Housman, Stoppard replied: "It's the Romantic/classicist contrast, isn't it, it's *Arcadia* again. I just realized there was something basically dramatic in the man who was two men." In *The Invention of Love*, Stoppard portrays Housman as *literally* two men, played by two different actors: the old man of seventy-seven at the end of his life (AEH) and the young man between the ages of eighteen and twenty-six (Housman). This bifocal vision structurally encapsulates the play's central thematic metaphor, a metaphor that will be dramatized in a number of significant ways in the play: the concept of the divided self.

In "Dream Song 205," poet John Berryman wrote of Housman: "he was a fork / saved by his double genius." Whether he was "saved" or not is one of the main issues raised by the play, but there is no question that Housman was indeed a "fork." On the most obvious level, Housman was bifurcated in terms of profession: he was both a scholar and a poet, as the opening lines of the play immediately establish. The ferryman Charon is waiting patiently to transport two dead souls across the river Styx for the underworld:

> CHARON. A poet and a scholar is what I was told.
> AEH. I think that must be me.
> CHARON. Both of them?
> AEH. I'm afraid so.
> CHARON. It sounded like two different people.
> AEH. I know.   (p. 2)

As a classical scholar and a romantic poet, Housman was very much "two different people." The scholar was all "head"; a professor of Latin, Housman produced rigorous textual criticism which he regarded as a "science" (p. 38), the tools of which were "logic" (p. 79) and rationality: "scholarship is a small redress against the vast unreason of what is taken from us" (p. 71). The poet, by contrast, was all "heart"; the "peculiar function of poetry," Housman stated in a public lecture at Cambridge, was "to transfuse emotion—not to transmit thought."

The combination of scholarship and poetry in a single person could easily be regarded as an ideal balance rather than a conflict;

what made it "divisive" in Housman's case was that the head far outweighed the heart. Housman published only two slim volumes of verse during his lifetime, devoting the vast majority of his time to intellectual pursuits. Significantly, we never see him engaged in any way with his own poetry in *The Invention of Love*, and only a few snippets from a handful of his poems are actually cited in the text. But the relative meagerness of Housman's poetic output is not really the issue here; it is that the emotions that inspired his poetry were *confined* to his poetry rather than acted out in his life. If Housman's head (the classicist) outweighed his heart (the romantic), it is because the head was given full rein while the heart was intentionally repressed. As Auden noted in his poem "A. E. Housman": "Deliberately he chose the dry-as-dust, / Kept tears like dirty postcards in a drawer."

This is the true sense in which Housman was a "fork," a divided self: while his romantic sensibility was allowed to come out in poetry, the man himself was unable to "come out" in life. If "The laws of God, the laws of man," he writes in one of his poems, were determined to "make me dance as they desire," then Housman would refuse to dance. Eros played a cruel trick on Housman: it made the object of his desire a heterosexual man— Moses Jackson, whom he first met as an undergraduate at Oxford and continued to love, chastely and from afar, for the rest of his life. When Housman sent his beloved "Mo" a copy of *Last Poems* in 1922, he inscribed it from "a fellow who thinks more of you than anything in the world," and added, significantly, "you are largely responsible for my writing poetry." In *The Invention of Love*, Stoppard assesses the enormous cost of that emotional sublimation.

—Hersh Zeifman, "The Comedy of Eros: Stoppard in Love," *The Cambridge Companion to Tom Stoppard*, ed. Katherine E. Kelly, (Cambridge: Cambridge University Press, 2001): pp. 192–194.

CHARLES ISHERWOOD ON EMOTION VERSUS INTELLECT

[Charles Isherwood, *Variety*'s chief theater critic, believes that the story's emotionality is sometimes overshadowed by the play's intellectualness and lengthy exposition.]

The play is structured as a fantasia taking place in the mind of the deceased Housman, who begins it with a matter-of-fact observation of his strange new state. "I'm dead, then. Good." Noting the murk surrounding him, he adds, "And this is the stygian gloom one has heard so much about." This delicious opening scene, in which Housman is introduced to the famous Charon (Jeff Weiss, a bit overripe), is Stoppard at his best: as irreverent as it is erudite. It is also economical.

The first two qualities are hallmarks of the whole play, but the last one, alas, isn't. "The Invention of Love" contains scenes of great emotional power, but their effectiveness—the play's as a whole, really—is sometimes occluded by the overwhelming intellectual and historical scaffolding surrounding them. The complexity of the play's architecture is paralleled in Bob Crowley's clever and attractive but somewhat fussy design scheme, which occasionally distracts the viewer from a text that needs concentrated attention.

To be sure, much of this is necessary scene-setting for audiences unfamiliar with Housman's life and work, to say nothing of the philosophies of John Ruskin and Walter Pater, and the love poetry of Catullus and Propertius. Housman was studying classics at Oxford at a time when the cult of aestheticism surrounding Pater was approaching its height. As Stoppard illustrates, worship of all things Greek—notably male friendship—led to some rough passages for Pater, while his fellow classicists Ruskin, Benjamin Jowett and Mark Pattison, all comically depicted here, professed with varying degrees of sternness to abhor the practice of homosexuality, even if it was a hallmark of a culture they prized above all others.

Much of this intellectual window-dressing is lively and entertaining, although less would probably suffice for the play's purposes. To sweeten the pill, Stoppard leavens the scenes in which these chattering classicists expound their divergent philosophies with playful humor. O'Brien's cast punches up the playfulness, sometimes to an unnecessary degree, as if seeking to reassure the audience that discussions of the purposes of higher education and debates about the merits of the medieval vs. Renaissance periods really can be fun.

But the heart of the play depicts the young Housman's love for his classmate, Moses Jackson (David Harbour), and the delicate give and take between the elder and younger Housman. As the elder looks on at the beginnings of his lifelong affection for Jackson ("I would have died for you, but I didn't have the luck," is his mournful refrain), he converses with his younger self about poetry, life and scholarship. (...)

Stoppard shows us that Housman, too, suffered for the love he invented and transmuted into poetry. His emotional immolation may not have been due to a failure of courage, as Wilde accuses—"Your 'honor' is all shame and timidity and compliance," he says—but something more noble, and harder to understand in our more self-indulgent age. Perhaps he simply couldn't see beyond the vision of love that engorged his heart at a young age and fed his poetry until his death. A perfectionist in his scholarly career—laboring over the placement of a comma in a Latin text—he couldn't accept anything less than the ideal he had dreamed of. Life didn't put the commas in the right places so he set it aside, and got to work. (...)

—Charles Isherwood, *"The Invention of Love." Variety* 382, 7 (2–8 April 2001): pp. 28, 31.

Tom Stoppard

A Walk on the Water (teleplay; re-broadcast as *The Preservation of George Riley* in 1964; later revised as *Enter a Free Man* in 1968), 1963.

"Life, Times: Fragment," "Reunion," "The Story," (short stories), 1964.

The Dissolution of Dominic Boot (one-act radio play adapted for TV as *The Engagement* in 1970), 1964.

This Way Out With Samuel Boot (unproduced teleplay), 1964.

'M' is for Moon Among Other Things (one-act radio play), 1964.

Rosencrantz and Guildenstern Meet King Lear, (one-act verse burlesque; basis for *Rosencrantz and Guildenstern Are Dead* in 1966), 1964.

The Gamblers (one-act play), 1965.

A Paragraph for Mr. Blake (teleplay based on the "The Story"), 1965.

How Sir Dudley Lost the Empire (unproduced teleplay), 1965.

The Dales (daily radio serial; wrote five episodes), 1965.

Lord Malquist and Mr Moon (novel), 1966.

If You're Glad I'll Be Frank (radio play), 1966.

Tango (stage adaptation of Nicholas Bethell's translation of Slawomir Mrozek's play), 1966.

A Separate Peace (teleplay), 1966.

Rosencrantz and Guildenstern Are Dead (play; adapted for the screen in 1990), 1966.

A Student's Diary: An Arab in London (weekly radio serial; wrote 70 episodes), 1966-67.

Teeth (teleplay), 1967.

Another Moon Called Earth (teleplay), 1967.

Albert's Bridge (radio play), 1967.

Enter a Free Man (play; revision of his earlier teleplay, *A Walk on the Water*), 1968.

The Real Inspector Hound (play), 1968.

Neutral Ground (teleplay), 1968.

Where Are They Now? (radio play), 1970.

The Engagement (screenplay based on *The Dissolution of Dominic Boot*; televised, then released to cinema), 1970.

After Magritte (play), 1970.

Dogg's Our Pet (play; later combined with *The (15 Minute) Dogg's Troupe Hamlet* to become *Dogg's Hamlet*, 1979), 1971.

Jumpers (play), 1972.

One Pair of Eyes: Tom Stoppard Doesn't Know (television documentary), 1972.

Artist Descending a Staircase (radio play; adapted as a play in 1988), 1972.

The House of Bernarda Alba (adaptation of Geferico Garcia Lorca's play), 1973.

Born Yesterday (play by Garson Kanin; directed by Tom Stoppard), 1973.

Travesties (play), 1974.

Eleventh House (teleplay; cowritten with Clive Exton), 1975.

The Boundary (teleplay; cowritten with Clive Exton), 1975.

The Romantic Englishwoman (screenplay; cowritten with Thomas Wiseman and based on his novel), 1975.

Three Men in a Boat (teleplay; based on the novel by Jerome K. Jerome; adapted for radio in 1994), 1975.

Dirty Linen and New-Found-Land (two one-act plays that are performed together), 1976.

The (15 Minute) Dogg's Troupe Hamlet (play; later combined with *Dogg's Our Pet* to become *Dogg's Hamlet*, 1979), 1976.

Every Good Boy Deserves Favour: A Play for Actors and Orchestra (play with orchestration; music by André Previn), 1977.

Professional Foul (teleplay), 1977.

Despair (screenplay; based on Valadimir Nabokov's novel), 1978.

Night and Day (play), 1978.

Dogg's Hamlet, Cahoot's Macbeth (one-act plays that are performed together), 1979.

Undiscovered Country (play; translation of Arthur Schnitzler's *Das Weite Land*), 1979.

The Human Factor (screenplay; based on Graham Greene's novel), 1979.

Acting (untitled stage documentary), 1980.

On the Razzle (play adapted from Johann Nestroy's *Einen Jux will er sich machen*), 1981.

The Real Thing (play), 1982.

The Dog It Was That Died (radio play; adapted for TV in 1988), 1982.

The Love for Three Oranges (translation of libretto for Prokofiev's opera), 1983.

Squaring the Circle (teleplay), 1984.

Rough Crossing (play; adapted from Ferenc Molnár's *Play at the Castle*), 1984.

Brazil (screenplay; cowritten by Terry Gilliam and Charles McKeown), 1985.

Dalliance (play adapted from Arnold Schnitzler's translation of *Liebelei*), 1986.

Largo Desolato: A Play in Seven Scenes (translation of Václav Havel's play), 1987.

Empire of the Sun (screenplay; based on J. G. Ballard's novel), 1987.

Hapgood (play), 1988.

A Far Off Place (unproduced screenplay; based on Laurens van der Post's novel), 1988.

Indiana Jones and the Last Crusade (screenplay; uncredited re-write), 1989.

Always (screenplay; uncredited re-write), 1989.

The Russia House (screenplay; based on John Le Carré's novel), 1990.

Rosencrantz and Guildenstern are Dead (screenplay; adapted from his 1966 play; directed by Tom Stoppard), 1990.

In the Native State (radio play; adapted for the stage as *Indian Ink* in 1995), 1991.

Billy Bathgate (screenplay; based on E. L. Doctorow's novel), 1991.

Arcadia (play; adapted for radio in 1993 or 1994), 1993.

Hopeful Monsters (unproduced screenplay; based on the novel by Nicholas Mosley), 1993.

The Merry Widow (new English narration for Franz Lehár's opera), 1993.

Cats (unproduced screenplay; animated version of Andrew Lloyd Webber's musical), 1994.

Indian Ink (play revised from the 1991 radio play, *In the Native State*), 1995.

The Invention of Love (play), 1997.

Poodle Springs (teleplay; adapted from the novel by Robert B. Parker; based on characters created by Raymond Chandler), 1998.

Shakespeare in Love (screenplay; cowritten by Marc Norman), 1998.

Enigma (screenplay; based on Robert Harris' novel), 1999.

Sleepy Hollow (screenplay; uncredited re-write), 1999.

Vatel (screenplay; cowritten by Jeanne Labrune), 2000.

The Seagull (play; adaptation of Anton Chekov's play), 2001.

K-19: The Widowmaker (screenplay; uncredited re-write), 2002.

The Coast of Utopia (a trilogy of sequential but self-contained plays: *Voyage*, *Shipwreck* and *Salvage*, produced by the National Theatre), 2002.

Tom Stoppard

Alwes, Derek B. "'Oh, Phooey to Death!': Boethian Consolation in Tom Stoppard's *Arcadia.*" *Papers on Language & Literature* 36 (2000): pp. 393–404

Andretta, Richard A. *Tom Stoppard, An Analytical Study of His Plays.* New Delhi: Har-Anand Publications in Association with Vikas Pub. House, 1992.

Bareham, T, ed. *Tom Stoppard:* Rosencrantz and Guildenstern are Dead, Jumpers, Travesties: *A Casebook.* Casebook Series. London: Macmillan Education, Ltd., 1990.

Bigsby, C. W. E. *Tom Stoppard.* Ed. Ian Scott-Kilvert. Harlow [Eng.]: Published for the British Council by Longman Group, 1976.

Bigsby, C.W.E., associate editor. *Contemporary English Drama.* New York: Holmes & Meier Publishers, 1981.

Billington, Michael. *Stoppard, the Playwright.* London and New York: Methuen, 1987.

Bloom, Harold, ed. *Tom Stoppard.* Modern Critical Views Series. New York: Chelsea House, 1986.

Brassell, Tim. *Tom Stoppard: An Assessment.* New York: St. Martin's Press, 1985.

Bratt, David. *Tom Stoppard: A Reference Guide.* A Reference Guide to Literature Series. Boston, Mass.: G.K. Hall, 1982.

Brustein, Robert. "On Theater: Popular Elitism" *New Republic* 213 (17 & 24 July 1995): pp. 36–38.

Cahn, Victor L. *Beyond Absurdity: The Plays of Tom Stoppard.* Cranbury, N.J.: Associated University Presses, Inc., 1979.

Colby, Douglas. *As the Curtain Rises: On Contemporary British Drama, 1966–1976.* Rutherford, N.J.: Fairleigh Dickinson University Press, 1978.

Corballis, Richard. *Stoppard: The Mystery and the Clockwork.* New York: Methuen, 1984.

Crump, G. B. "The Universe as Murder Mystery: Tom Stoppard's *Jumpers*" *Contemporary Literature* 20 (1979): 354–386.

Dean, Joan Fitzpatrick. *Tom Stoppard: Comedy as a Moral Matrix*. A Literary Frontiers Edition Series. Columbia: University of Missouri Press, 1981.

Delaney, Paul, ed. *Tom Stoppard in Conversation*. Ann Arbor: The University of Michigan Press, 1994.

Delaney, Paul. *Tom Stoppard: The Moral Vision of the Major Plays*. Houndmills, Basingstoke, Hampshire [Eng.]: Macmillan, 1990.

Delaney, Paul. *Tom Stoppard: The Moral Vision of the Major Plays*. New York: St. Martin's Press, 1990.

Egan, Robert. "A Thin Beam of Light: The Purpose of Playing in *Rosencrantz and Guildenstern Are Dead*" *Theatre Journal* 31 (1979): pp. 59–69

Fleming, John. *Stoppard's Theatre: Finding Order Amid Chaos*. Literary Modernism Series. Austin: University of Texas Press, 2001.

Gabbard, Lucina Paquet. *The Stoppard Plays*. Troy, N.Y.: Whitston Pub. Co., 1982.

Gordon, Robert. *Rosencrantz and Guildenstern Are Dead, Jumpers*, and *The Real Thing*. Text and Performance Series. Houndmills, Basingstoke, Hampshire [Eng.]: Macmillan, 1991.

Gussow, Mel. *Conversations with Stoppard*. 1st Limelight edition. New York: Limelight Editions, 1995.

Harty, John III, ed. *Tom Stoppard : A Casebook*. Garland Reference Library of the Humanities Series, vol. 794, Casebooks on Modern Dramatists, vol. 1. New York: Garland, 1988.

Hayman, Ronald. *Tom Stoppard*. Revised Fourth Edition. Totowa, NJ: Rowman and Littlefield, 1982.

Hayman, Ronald. *Tom Stoppard*. Revised Third Edition. Totowa, NJ: Rowman and Littlefield, 1979.

Hayman, Ronald. *Tom Stoppard*. Totowa, NJ: Rowman and Littlefield, 1977.

Heilpern, John. *"The Invention of Love* is a Many-Splendored Thing." *The New York Observer* (9 April 2001): pp. 28.

Hu, Stephen. *Tom Stoppard's Stagecraft.* American University Studies Series IV, *English Language and Literature* v. 78. New York: P. Lang, 1989.

Hunter, Jim. *A Faber Critical Guide: Tom Stoppard: Rosencrantz and Guildenstern Are Dead, Jumpers, Travesties, Arcadia.* London: Faber and Faber, 2000.

Hunter, Jim. *Tom Stoppard's Plays.* London: Faber and Faber, 1982.

H?rková, Klára. *Mirror Images: A Comparison of the Early Plays of Václav Havel and Tom Stoppard with Special Reference to Their Political Aspects.* Aachen British and American Studies Series, vol. 14. Frankfurt am Main [Ger.] and New York: P. Lang, 2000.

Isherwood, Charles. *"The Invention of Love" Variety* 382 (2-8 April 2001): pp. 28–31.

Jenkins, Anthony, ed. *Critical Essays on Tom Stoppard.* Boston, Mass.: G.K. Hall, 1990.

Jenkins, Anthony. *The Theatre of Tom Stoppard.* Second edition. Cambridge and New York: Cambridge University Press, 1989.

Jenkins, Anthony. *The Theatre of Tom Stoppard.* Cambridge and New York: Cambridge University Press, 1987.

Kelly, Katherine E., ed. *The Cambridge Companion to Tom Stoppard.* Cambridge and New York: Cambridge University Press, 2001.

Kelly, Katherine E. *Tom Stoppard and the Craft of Comedy: Medium and Genre at Play.* Theater: Text/Theory/Performance Series. Ann Arbor, Mich.: University of Michigan Press, 1991.

King, Kimball. *Twenty Modern British Playwrights: A Bibliography, 1956 to 1976.* New York: Garland, 1977.

Londré, Felicia Hardison. *Tom Stoppard.* Modern Literature Series. New York: F. Ungar Pub. Co., 1981.

Melbourne, Lucy. "'Plotting the Apple of Knowledge': Tom Stoppard's *Arcadia* as Iterated Theatrical Algorithm." *Modern Drama* 41 (1998): pp. 557–57.

Page, Malcolm, ed. *File on Stoppard*. Writer-Files Series. London and New York: Methuen, 1986.

Peter, John. "*The Invention of Love* is Tom Stoppard at His Best: Manipulative, Inquisitive, Irresistible. John Peter Sees a Master at Work" *The Sunday Times* 9,032 (5 October 1997): pp. 8–9.

Robinson, Gabrielle Scott. "Plays Without Plot: The Theatre of Tom Stoppard." *Educational Theatre Journal* 29 (1977): pp. 37–48.

Rusinko, Susan. *Tom Stoppard*. Twayne's English Authors Series. Boston: Twayne Publishers, 1986.

Ryan, Carrie. "Translating *The Invention of Love*: The Journey From Page to Stage For Tom Stoppard's Latest Play." *Journal of Modern Literature* 24 (Winter 2000–2001): pp. 197–204.

Sammells, Neil. *Tom Stoppard: The Artist as Critic*. New York: St. Martin's, 1988.

Scott-Kivert, Ian, ed. *British Writers: Supplement I, Graham Greene to Tom Stoppard*. New York: Scribner, 1987.

Tan, Peter K. W. *A Stylistics of Drama: With Special Focus on Stoppard's* Travesties. Singapore: Singapore University Press, National University of Singapore, 1993.

Tynan, Kenneth. *Show People: Profiles in Entertainment*. New York: Simon and Schuster, 1979.

Whitaker, Thomas R. *Tom Stoppard*. Grove Press Modern Dramatists Series. New York: Grove Press, 1983.

Zarhy-Levo, Yael. *The Theatrical Critic as Cultural Agent: Constructing Pinter, Orton and Stoppard as Absurdist Playwrights*. Artists and Issues in the Theatre Series, vol. 12. New York: Peter Lang Pub., 2001.

ACKNOWLEDGMENTS

Tom Stoppard by C. W. E Bigsby, ed. Ian Scott-Kilvert (Harlow [Eng.]: Published for the British Council by Longman Group, 1976): pp. 15–16. © 1976 by The Longman Group. Reprinted by permission.

"A Thin Beam of Light: The Purpose of Playing in *Rosencrantz and Guildenstern Are Dead*" by Robert Egan. From *Theatre Journal* 31, 1 (1979): pp. 62, 66–67, 69. © 1979 by *Theatre Journal*. Reprinted by permission.

The Stoppard Plays by Lucina Paquet Gabbard (Troy, N.Y.: Whitston Pub. Co., 1982): pp. 33–36, 37, 92–95. © 1982 by Whitston Publishing Co. Reprinted by permission.

Stoppard, the Mystery and the Clockwork by Richard Corballis (New York: Methuen, 1984): pp. 35–36, 42–43, 44–47, 64–67, 73–75, 76, 80–82, 92–94. © 1984 by Methuen. Reprinted by permission.

Tom Stoppard: The Artist as Critic by Neil Sammells (New York: St. Martin's, 1988): pp. 37–38. © 1988 by Neil Sammells. Reprinted with permission of Palgrave Macmillan.

"The Universe as Murder Mystery: Tom Stoppard's *Jumpers*" by G. B. Crump. From *Contemporary Literature* 20, 3 (1979): pp. 366–368. © 1979 by *Contemporary Literature*. Reprinted by permission of the University of Wisconsin Press.

The Theatre of Tom Stoppard by Anthony Jenkins (Cambridge: Cambridge University Press, 1987): pp. 92–95, 123–124. © 1987 by Cambridge University Press. Reprinted with the permission of Cambridge University Press.

Tom Stoppard: The Moral Vision of the Major Plays by Paul Delaney (New York: St. Martin's Press, 1990): pp. 39–40, 41–42, 43, 45–46, 62–63, 65–67, 70, 77, 79, 81. © 1990 by Paul Delaney. Reprinted with permission of Palgrave Macmillan.

Tom Stoppard and the Craft of Comedy: Medium and Genre at Play by Katherine E. Kelly (Ann Arbor, Mich.: University of Michigan Press, 1991): pp. 102–104. © 1991 by University of Michigan Press. Reprinted by permission.

Tom Stoppard: An Assessment by Tim Brassell (New York: St. Martin's Press, 1985): pp. 140–141, 158–161, 162. © 1985 by Tim Brassell. Reprinted with permission of Palgrave Macmillan.

Tom Stoppard by Susan Rusinko, Twayne's English Authors Series, (Boston: Twayne Publishers, 1986): pp. 46, 47, 51–52, 56. © 1986 by Twayne Publishers. Reprinted by permission of The Gale Group.

"'Plotting the Apple of Knowledge': Tom Stoppard's *Arcadia* as Iterated Theatrical Algorithm" by Lucy Melbourne. From *Modern Drama* 41, 4 (1998): pp. 557, 560, 568–569, 569–570. © 1998 by Modern Drama. Reprinted by permission.

"'Oh, Phooey to Death!'": Boethian Consolation in Tom Stoppard's *Arcadia*" by Derek B. Alwes. From *Papers on Language & Literature* 36, 4 (2000): pp. 401–403. © 2000 by *Papers on Language & Literature*. Reprinted by permission.

"Science in *Hapgood* and *Arcadia*" by Paul Edwards. From *The Cambridge Companion to Tom Stoppard*, ed. Katherine E. Kelly, (Cambridge: Cambridge University Press, 2001): pp. 179–180, 182–183. © 2001 by Cambridge University Press. Reprinted with the permission of Cambridge University Press.

Stoppard's Theatre: Finding Order Amid Chaos by John Fleming, Literary Modernism Series, (Austin: University of Texas Press, 2001): pp. 200–205, 239–242. © 2001 by the University of Texas Press. Reprinted by permission of the University of Texas Press.

"The Comedy of Eros: Stoppard in Love" by Hersh Zeifman. From *The Cambridge Companion to Tom Stoppard*, ed. Katherine E. Kelly, (Cambridge: Cambridge University Press, 2001): pp. 187–190, 192–194. © 2001 by Cambridge University Press. Reprinted with the permission of Cambridge University Press.

"*The Invention of Love* is Tom Stoppard at His Best: Manipulative, Inquisitive, Irresistible. John Peter Sees a Master at Work" by John Peter. From *The Sunday Times* 9,032 (October 5, 1997): pp. 11–8–11–9. © 1997 by *The Sunday Times*. Reprinted by permission.

11, 126–138; Robinson Ellis in, 117, 123; emotion versus intellect in, 136–138; Frank Harris in, 118–119, 124, 129–131; Housman as scholar and poet in, 134–136; Housman in, 115–124, 126–129, 137–138; Katherine "Kate" Housman in, 117, 121, 123, 128; Housman versus Wilde in, 130–134; Moses John "Jo" Jackson in, 115–122, 124–127, 129, 131–133, 136, 138; Jerome K. Jerome in, 119–120, 124, 129–130; Benjamin Jowett in, 115–116, 123, 137; Henry Labouchere in, 118–119, 123, 130–131; Walter Pater in, 115–116, 122–123, 137; Mark Pattison in, 115–116, 122, 128, 137; plot summary of, 115–120; Alfred Williams Pollard in, 115–116, 118, 120, 122; John Percival Postgate in, 119, 124; John Ruskin in, 115–116, 123, 129, 137; W.T. Stead in, 118–119, 124, 130–131; Oscar Wilde in, 115–116, 118–125, 129, 138

JUMPERS, 38–67; Inspector Bones in, 40–41, 44, 47–48, 51, 57, 61; characters in, 43–45, Sam Clegthorpe in, 39, 42–43, 45, 50, 54–55; critical views on, 15, 46–67, 80, 87; Crouch in, 38, 41–42, 44, 51, 53; Sir Archibald Jump or "Archie," 38–44, 47–48, 50–60, 62, 65–66; The Jumpers in, 38–40, 42–46, 49, 51–53, 55–56, 61–63; Duncan McFee in, 40–42, 44–48, 50–52, 54, 61–62; the Moore's emotional separateness in, 56–60; Dorothy "Dotty" Moore in, 15, 38–44, 46–52, 56–60, 63–67; George Moore in, 38–45, 49–50, 56–61, 63; George Moore's failures in, 46–48; George Moore's faith in intuition in, 52–56; moral absolution in, 61–64; moral relativism in, 61–64; plot summary of, 38–42; the role of the Coda in, 65–67; Captain Horatio Scott in, 42, 45, 52, 54; The Secretary in, 38, 41, 42, 44, 61; symbolism of the characters in, 48–52

LORD MALQUIST AND MR. MOON, 14

ROSENCRANTZ AND GUILDENSTERN ARE DEAD, 17–37; absurdity in, 24–25; Alfred in, 17, 23, 30; characters in, 22–23; Claudius in, 17–20, 22, 26, 31–35; conflicting views of art in, 35–37; contrast between Ros and Guil and the Tragedians in, 29–34; critical views on, 11, 14, 24–37, 56, 113; death theme in, 25–29; Gertrude in, 17–18, 21, 23; Guildenstern in, 22–23, 25–37, 66; Hamlet in, 17–23, 25–33, 35–36; Ophelia in, 18, 21, 23; The Player in, 17–20, 22, 26, 31–35; plot summary of, 17–21; Polonius in, 18–19, 21, 23; Rosencrantz in, 17–23, 25–36